UNIVERSIT
WIN

Martial Rose Library
Tel: 01962 827306

Classical World Series

Aristophanes and his Theatre of the Absurd, Paul Cartledge
Art and the Romans, Anne Haward
Athens and Sparta, S. Todd
Athens under Tyrants, J. Smith
Athletics in the Ancient World, Zahra Newby
Attic Orators, Michael Edwards
Augustan Rome, Andrew Wallace-Hadrill
Cicero and the End of the Roman Republic, Thomas Wiedemann
Cities of Roman Italy, Guy de la Bédoyère
Classical Archaeology in the Field, S. J. Hill, L. Bowkett and
K. & D. Wardle
Classical Epic: Homer and Virgil, Richard Jenkyns
Democracy in Classical Athens, Christopher Carey
Early Greek Lawgivers, John Lewis
Environment and the Classical World, Patricia Jeskins
Greece and the Persians, John Sharwood Smith
Greek and Roman Historians, Timothy E. Duff
Greek and Roman Medicine, Helen King
Greek Architecture, R. Tomlinson
Greek Literature in the Roman Empire, Jason König
Greek Sculpture, Georgina Muskett
Greek Tragedy: Themes and Contexts, Laura Swift
Greek Vases, Elizabeth Moignard
Homer: The Iliad, William Allan
Julio-Claudian Emperors, T. Wiedemann
Lucretius and the Didactic Epic, Monica Gale

Periclean Athens

P. J. Rhodes

Bloomsbury Academic
An imprint of Bloomsbury Publishing Plc

B L O O M S B U R Y
LONDON · OXFORD · NEW YORK · NEW DELHI · SYDNEY

Bloomsbury Academic

An imprint of Bloomsbury Publishing Plc

50 Bedford Square   1385 Broadway
London   New York
WC1B 3DP   NY 10018
UK   USA

www.bloomsbury.com

**BLOOMSBURY and the Diana logo are trademarks of
Bloomsbury Publishing Plc**

First published 2018

© P. J. Rhodes, 2018

P. J. Rhodes has asserted his right under the Copyright, Designs and
Patents Act, 1988, to be identified as Author of this work.

British Library Cataloguing-in-Publication Data
A catalogue record for this book is available from the British Library.

ISBN: PB: 978-1-3500-1495-4
ePDF: 978-1-3500-1497-8
eBook: 978-1-3500-1496-1

Library of Congress Cataloging-in-Publication Data
A catalog record for this book is available from the Library of Congress.

Cover design: Terry Woodley
Cover image © f11photo/Shutterstock

Typeset by Deanta Global Publishing Services, Chennai, India
Printed and bound in India

To find out more about our authors and books visit www.bloomsbury.com.
Here you will find extracts, author interviews, details of forthcoming
events and the option to sign up for our newsletters.

Contents

List of Illustrations

Maps

Figures

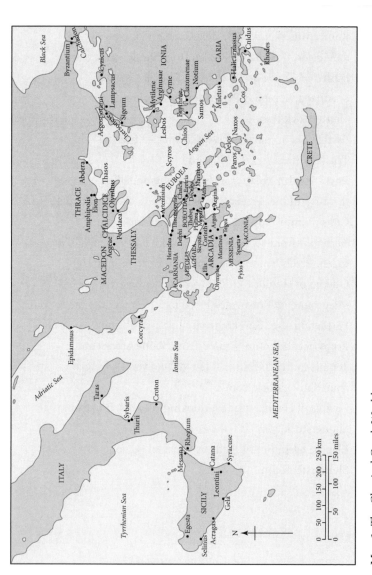

Map 1 The Classical Greek World.

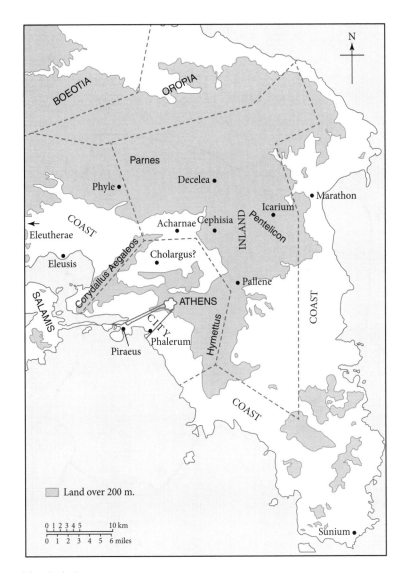

N

BOEOTIA

OROPIA

Parnes

Phyle •

Decelea •

• Marathon

Icarium

COAST

Acharnae Cephisia

Pentelicon

Eleutherae

INLAND

Eleusis •

Cholargus? •

SALAMIS

Corydallus Aegaleos

Pallene •

ATHENS

COAST

Piraeus

Phalerum

Hymettus

COAST

Land over 200 m.

0 1 2 3 4 5   10 km
0 1 2 3 4 5 6 miles

Sunium •

Map 2 Attica.

(Names of demes are in seriffed capital and lower case letters; names of Cleisthenes' three regions are in seriffed capitals. Regional boundaries are purely schematic.)

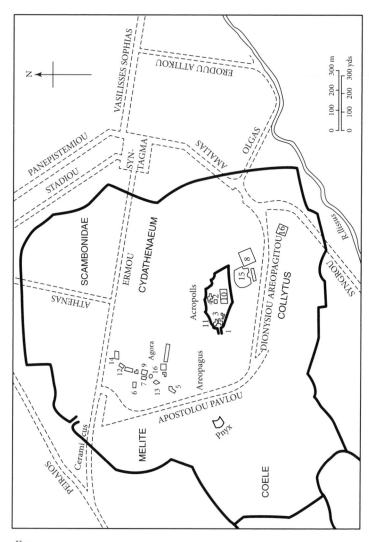

Key

1	Athena Nike, temple of	9	Old Bouleuterion = Metroum
2	Athena, Old temple of	10	Parthenon
3	Athena Promachos, statue of	11	Propylaea
4	Erechtheum	12	Stoa of the Basileus
5	Gaol (?)	13	Strategion (?)
6	Hephaestus, temple of	14	Stoa Poikile
7	New Bouleuterion	15	Theatre of Dionysus
8	Odeion	16	Tholos

Map 3 Plan of Athens.

Names of demes are in sanserif capital letters; principal modern streets are shown in pecked lines.

Preface

My thanks to Ms A. Wright for inviting me to contribute this book to Bloomsbury's Classical World Series, which is intended primarily for students in schools and the earlier years of university courses and for their teachers, and to all those involved in its production, including the publishers' advisers and those who have given permission for the use of copyright illustrations. My thanks also to Dr S. English, for again impersonating a reader of the kind envisaged and helping me to improve on a first draft.

The subject is one in which there is room for disagreement, about some of the facts, and about the interpretation even of agreed facts. What I present here is my own view: I have tried to play fair, to distinguish facts from interpretations and to give notice where what I say is particularly open to dispute, but I have not qualified with 'probably' every statement which could be so qualified.

There are different ways of rendering Greek words and names in the Latin alphabet: I normally use anglicized or latinized forms for words and names printed in ordinary roman type (e.g. acropolis, Athens, drachmae, Pericles) but direct transliteration for words printed in italics (e.g. *ekklesia*, *proxenos*). As for pronunciation, the one rule that matters is that *e* after a consonant does not modify the previous vowel but forms part of a new syllable: thus the word *time*, 'honour', is of two syllables (its ancient pronunciation approximated to *tee-meh*).

References to Ancient Texts

Here as everywhere in ancient history the evidence available to us is patchy, and we have to make the most (but avoid making too much) of what we have. For a book of this kind I have judged it best not to provide a great weight of citations, but to give the main references selectively. The one narrative by a contemporary is the history of Thucydides: Books II–VIII cover the history of the Peloponnesian War, from its outbreak in 431 until the account breaks off unfinished in 411; Book I deals with the circumstances leading to the outbreak of the war and includes in chs. 89–118 and 128–38 digressions on earlier events from 478 onwards. Other fifth-century material includes: tragedies and comedies by Athenian playwrights; a pamphlet on the *Athenian Constitution*, probably of the 420s, preserved with the works of Xenophon but by an unknown author often referred to as the 'Old Oligarch'; also texts inscribed on stone, often incompletely preserved and of uncertain date. Many later works, of varying nature, varying dates and varying reliability, refer to this period: for those cited in this book, see the list of abbreviations below.

There are Loeb Classical Library editions (Harvard University Press; originally published jointly with London: Heinemann), with original text and English translation, of all the literary texts cited here apart from some of which only 'fragments' quoted in other works survive. There are other English translations, for example in the Oxford World's Classics (Oxford University Press) and the Penguin Classics (London: Penguin) series, of many of them. In Plutarch's *Lives*, I divide the chapters into sections in accordance with the Budé (Collection des Universités de France. Paris: Les Belles Lettres) and Teubner (Leipzig: Teubner, now Berlin: de Gruyter) editions; the Loeb edition divides the chapters into fewer, larger sections.

In references to inscriptions and a few other texts, 'A = B ~ C' indicates that A and B give an original text of the same inscription or

passage but not necessarily identical versions of it, and that C gives an English translation of a version of that text.
I use the following abbreviations.

Authors and *Works*

Aesch.		Aeschylus, tragedian, C5
	Supp.	*Supplices* (*Suppliant Women*)
Antiph.		Antiphon, rhetorician, C5
Ar.		Aristophanes, comedian, C5–4
	Ach.	*Acharnenses* (*Acharnians*)
	Nub.	*Nubes* (*Clouds*)
	schol.	scholiast (ancient commentary)
Arist.		Aristotle, philosopher and polymath, C4
	Poet.	*Poetics*
	Pol.	*Politics*
	Rhet.	*Rhetoric*
Ath. Pol.		*Athenaion Politeia* (*Athenian Constitution*)
		(when cited without author, reference is to the work of this title written in Aristotle's school)
Dem.		Demosthenes, orator and politician, C4
Diod. Sic.		Diodorus Siculus (of Sicily), historian, C1
Diog. Laert.		Diogenes Laertius, C3 AD, biographer of philosophers
Duris		Duris, C4–3, historian
Hdt.		Herodotus, C5, historian
Idomeneus		Idomeneus, C4–3, biographer
Lyc.		Lycurgus, C4, orator and politician
	Leocr.	*Against Leocrates*
Paus.		Pausanias, C2 AD, traveller
Philoch.		Philochorus, C4–3, historian
Pind.		Pindar, C5, poet
	Pyth.	*Pythians*
Pl.		Plato, C4, philosopher

Grg.	*Gorgias*
Hp. Mai.	*Hippias Maior* [there is also a *Hippias Minor*]
Meno	*Meno*
Prt.	*Protagoras*
Resp.	*Res Publica* (*Republic*)

Plin.   Pliny the elder, C1 AD, polymath
  H.N.   *Historia Naturalis* (*Natural History*)
Plut.   Plutarch, C1–2 AD, writer on biography and other subjects

Alc.	*Alcibiades*
Arist.	*Aristides*
Cim.	*Cimon*
Nic.	*Nicias*
Per.	*Pericles*
Sol.	*Solon*
Them.	*Themistocles*

[Plut.] *X Or.*   *Lives of the Ten Orators*, preserved with the works of
           Plutarch
Solon   Solon, C6, poet and politician
           cited from M. L. West, *Iambi et Elegi Graeci* (Oxford
           University Press, 2nd ed., 1989–92)
Thuc.   Thucydides, C5, historian
Xen.   Xenophon, C5–4, writer on history and other subjects
[Xen.]   *Ath. Pol. Athenaion Politeia* (*Athenian Constitution*),
           preserved with the works of Xenophon

Collections of Texts

FGrH   F. Jacoby et al., *Die Fragmente der griechischen Historiker*
           (Berlin: Weidmann → Leiden: Brill, 1926–). I. Worthington
           (ed.), *Brill's New Jacoby* (Leiden: Brill, on line 2007–),
           includes English translations.

Fornara   C. W. Fornara, *Translated Documents of Greece and Rome,* i. *Archaic Times to the End of the Peloponnesian War* (Cambridge University Press, 2nd edition, 1983).

Harding   P. Harding, *Translated Documents of Greece and Rome,* ii. *From the End of the Peloponnesian War to the Battle of Ipsus* (Cambridge University Press, 1985).

IG   *Inscriptiones Graecae.*

    i^3 vol. i, 3rd edition.

    ii^2 vol. ii, 2nd edition.

M&L   R. Meiggs & D. M. Lewis, *A Selection of Greek Historical Inscriptions to the End of the Fifth Century* BC (Oxford University Press, 1969; reprinted with *addenda* 1988).

O&R   R. G. Osborne & P. J. Rhodes, *Greek Historical Inscriptions, 478–404* BC (Oxford University Press, 2017; includes translations).

R&O   P. J. Rhodes & R. G. Osborne, *Greek Historical Inscriptions, 404–323* BC (Oxford University Press, 2003, corrected reprint 2007; includes translations).

Vorsokr.   H. Diels, revised by W. Kranz, *Die Fragmente der Vorsokratiker* (Berlin: Weidmann, 6th edition 1951). K. Freeman, *Ancilla to the Pre-Socratic Philosophers* (Oxford: Blackwell, 1952), translates the fragments.

Principal Dates

Dates in the form 478/7 are years, usually Athenian official years, which began about July, and 47<u>8</u>/7 and 478/<u>7</u> denote the earlier and the later part of the year respectively. The formulation 478–477 denotes a period spanning the Julian years 478 and 477. Greeks did not count years in that way, but where there was a monarchic ruler years were numbered as years of his reign. In other cities they were identified by the name of an 'eponymous' official: in Athens this was the archon; e.g. 478/7 was the year when Timosthenes was archon. Items particularly relevant to Pericles are printed in **bold** type.

630s/620s	Cylon's bid for tyranny
621/0	legislation of Draco
594/3	archonship and reforms of Solon
c. 561/0	first *coup* of Pisistratus
c. 556	second *coup* of Pisisitratus
546/5	third *coup* of Pisistratus
528/7	death of Pisistratus
51<u>4</u>/3	assassination of Hipparchus
511/0	expulsion of Hippias
508/7	reforms of Cleisthenes
498–493	Ionian Revolt
c. 498–494	**birth of Pericles**
490	first Persian invasion of Greece: battle of Marathon
485/<u>4</u>	**Xanthippus ostracized**
480–479	second Persian invasion of Greece: battles of Thermopylae and Artemisium, Salamis, Plataea, Mycale
478/7	foundation of Delian League
473/<u>2</u>	**Pericles *choregos* for Aeschylus**
462/1	reforms of Ephialtes, ostracism of Cimon
c. 460–454	campaign in Egypt

c. 460–446	First Peloponnesian War
454	Delian League treasury moved to Athens
451/0	**Pericles' law on Athenian citizenship**
447/6	beginning of building work on acropolis
446/5	Thirty Years' Peace between Athens and Sparta
444/3 (?)	foundation of Thurii
c. 444/<u>3</u>	ostracism of Thucydides, son of Melesias
440–439	war against Samos
438/7	**trials of Pheidias and of Pericles**
437/6	foundation of Amphipolis
433	Athenian involvement in war between Corinth and Corcyra
432	revolt of Potidaea
431	outbreak of Peloponnesian War
430–426	plague at Athens
430	**Pericles deposed from generalship, but re-elected for next year**
429	**death of Pericles**
421	Peace of Nicias
415–413	expedition to Sicily
411–410	régimes of Four Hundred and of Five Thousand
404	end of Peloponnesian War
404–403	régime of Thirty
387/<u>6</u>	King's Peace
378/7	foundation of Second Athenian League
371	defeat of Sparta by Thebes at Leuctra
356–355	Social War
338	defeat of Athens and Thebes by Philip of Macedon at Chaeronea
321	overthrow of Athenian democracy by Macedon

1

Pericles and His City

Athens and the Greek world

In the second and third quarters of the fifth century BC, Pericles was one of the most prominent politicians in Athens, at a time when Athens was one of the most powerful politically and militarily, and one of the most flourishing and influential culturally, of the thousand or so *poleis* (singular *polis*: translated 'city', but many were not as large or as urbanized as that word would suggest) in the Greek world. That world extended beyond the Greek heartland of mainland Greece, the Aegean Sea and western Asia Minor (in present-day Turkey), to the west as far as mainland Italy and Sicily, with a few Greek settlements still farther west, and to the east as far as the northern and southern shores of Asia Minor, and around the rest of the shores of the Black Sea and in Cyprus. The fifth and fourth centuries are commonly regarded as the 'classical' period of ancient Greece, following the 'archaic' period in which Greece developed from the comparatively primitive 'dark age' around 1000, and preceding the 'hellenistic' period after the death of Alexander the Great of Macedon in 323, in which, thanks to Alexander's conquests, the Greek world extended into the Near and Middle East and the major powers were kingdoms formed out of parts of his empire.

Classical Greece is well worth studying, for its achievements of various kinds which have had an ongoing influence; and classical Athens is worth studying, for its particular achievements, and because one result of its position in the Greece of its time is that a large proportion of the material which enables us to study classical Greece is Athenian or connected in some way with Athens. We should not accept uncritically the view found in some fourth-century texts that (the period which we call) the fifth century was a time of greatness while the fourth century fell short of it; but it is not only because of the words which Thucydides attributed to Pericles in his funeral oration of 431/0 (Thuc. II. 36–46) that the fifth century can be regarded as a period of greatness for Greece and for Athens. Pericles was not as powerful within Athens as Thucydides wanted his readers to think, but he can be associated with much that Athens did, in various spheres, during his career, and so there is good reason for this book about Athens in the middle of the fifth century to bear the title *Periclean Athens*.

Although it contains some biographical material, particularly in this chapter, this is a book about Periclean Athens, not a biography of Pericles. Although Plutarch (writing about AD 100) included Pericles in his *Parallel Lives* of famous Greeks and famous Romans (Pericles' Roman counterpart is Q. Fabius Maximus, the 'delayer' who fought against Hannibal of Carthage in the third century BC), using material from various sources of varying quality, the material does not exist which would be needed to write a satisfactory biography of Pericles.

Athens was far from being a typical Greek city. About 80 per cent of the thousand or so cities in the classical Greek world had a territory of not more than 200 square kilometres (77 square miles), whereas only thirteen had more than 1,000 square kilometres (385 square miles). Among those were Athens, with 2,600 square kilometres (1,000 square miles, the size of County Durham or Rhode Island), and Sparta, with 6,200 square kilometres (2,400 square miles, rather smaller than Devon or larger than Delaware), both larger than any other city on the Greek mainland.

Although there was a general similarity among the various Greek communities, each city aspired to run its own affairs, with its citizens enacting their own laws and deciding their own policies, and so within the overall similarity there were varieties of detail. Each city had its own calendar, though regularly based on a year of twelve lunar months with a thirteenth added in some years to keep the calendar in step with the seasons. Each city decided on its own weights, measures and, in many cases, coinage, though a city might for trading convenience choose to use the same standards as one of its neighbours. Athens' 'owl' coinage, struck from silver mined in the south-east of Attica – an important resource of classical Athens – with the head of the goddess Athena on the obverse and an owl, an olive branch and AΘE for Athens on the reverse (cf. fig. 1.1), in the fifth century became the most desirable currency in the Greek world; and probably in the 420s, after Pericles' death, Athens ordered the other states of its alliance the Delian League to use Athenian silver coinage and Athenian weights and measures (*IG* i³ 1453 = O&R 155 ~ Fornara 97).

In the polytheistic religion of the Greeks, there was general agreement on the principal gods (such as Zeus and Hera), and there were some sanctuaries with their festivals which had more than a local appeal (particularly that of Zeus at Olympia and that of Apollo at Delphi; Athens achieved that for its sanctuary of Demeter and Persephone at Eleusis), but in each city particular gods were particularly favoured, and there were distinctive local features of their cult. Athena in Athens was not exactly the same as Athena in Sparta, and indeed within Athens and Attica there were various sanctuaries of Athena, where she was worshipped under different cult titles with different rituals on different occasions. On religion, and also on philosophy, in Athens, see further Chapter 4.

Figure 1.1 4 drachmae 'owl' coin (*c.* 440–420).

There was always a tendency for larger cities to encroach on smaller and for smaller cities to resist that encroachment; and when there were several cities in a single geographical region various outcomes were possible. In Arcadia, in the centre of the Peloponnese (southern Greece), no one city predominated, though some smaller cities were made subordinate to larger neighbours. In Boeotia, in central Greece north of Athens, there were again several cities with some smaller ones subordinate to larger neighbours, but there was in addition a federal organization, in which Thebes was the strongest city but not always unchallenged, through which Boeotia as a single entity had dealings with the rest of the Greek world.

Sparta in the south of the Peloponnese had by *c.* 600 conquered the whole of its region of Laconia, and also Messenia to the west. The citizens (as always in the Greek world, free adult males) of Sparta ruled, and the other inhabitants became in some instances subordinates known as *perioikoi* ('those living around'), or in other instances slaves known as helots ('captives'). Athens similarly had come to control the whole region of Attica; but, while the town of Athens was the centre of government, and the local settlements had a subsidiary status, all the free adult male inhabitants were made citizens of Athens.

And, by the time of Pericles, both Sparta and Athens had gained power beyond their own regions. Sparta was unable to conquer the rest of the Peloponnese as it had conquered Messenia, but in the second half of the sixth century it gained power over the whole of the Peloponnese except the region of Achaea (in the north, separated by mountains from the rest and more involved with the area on the north side of the Gulf of Corinth) and the city of Argos (in the north-east, never willing to accept Spartan supremacy). These Peloponnesian cities were made allies of Sparta, and were expected to follow its lead in foreign policy. The resulting alliance was known at the time as The Lacedaemonians (i.e. Spartans) and Their Allies, and is often now referred to as the Peloponnesian League; probably there was not a fully worked-out organization from the beginning, but issues were addressed as they arose.

When the Greeks of western Asia Minor embarked on the Ionian Revolt against Persia (since the middle of the sixth century, the dominant power in the near east), in the 490s, they appealed to Sparta and Athens in particular for support, and Athens (and Eretria on the island of Euboea) sent some help. The revolt was suppressed, and the involvement of Athens and Eretria provided the Persians with an excuse for invading mainland Greece. In 490 they captured Eretria but were defeated by Athens (and its neighbour Plataea) at Marathon; Spartan support for Athens did not arrive until after the battle. In 480 the Persians sent larger forces in the hope of conquering the whole of mainland Greece, and Sparta was accepted as the leader of the cities which chose to unite in resistance (by no means all did). The Persians were successful at first, at Thermopylae on the Greek mainland and at Artemisium at sea, but they were defeated on sea at Salamis in 480 (Athens providing more than half of the total Greek fleet), and on land at Plataea (and at Mycale in Asia Minor) in 479.

We now know that the Persians never invaded Greece again, but after the war of 480–479 it seemed likely that they would. Fighting continued around the Aegean, at first under Spartan leadership, but the misconduct of the Spartan commander Pausanias led to the taking of the lead by Athens and the withdrawal of Sparta. The resulting Delian League (its modern name: the headquarters was originally on the sacred island of Delos) began as an alliance of independent cities but was gradually made subject to Athens in unprecedented ways and to an unprecedented extent, until it could fairly be described as an Athenian empire. As the historian Thucydides writes, 'the Athenians by becoming great and inspiring fear in the Spartans forced them to go to war' (Thuc. I. 23. vi). That war was the Peloponnesian War of 431–404: it was finally won by Sparta with help from Persia, but that did not resolve the rivalry between Sparta and Athens for long. On the empire and the Peloponnesian War, see further Chapter 3.

As for internal governance, there had been a general tendency across the Greek cities during the archaic period for régimes to develop in which power was not monopolized by an individual or a small clique but there was a plurality of officials appointed for short terms with restrictions on reappointment, and at any rate the most important decisions were entrusted to an assembly open to all qualified citizens (in some places the poorest were not qualified), whose proceedings were subject to more or less control by a smaller council which met more frequently. This pattern was regarded by the fourth-century philosopher Aristotle as characteristic of the self-government of a city by its citizens, and he referred to it as 'ruling and being ruled in turn' (Arist. *Pol.* I. 1259 B 4–6). In fifth-century Athens, this development was taken to a considerable extent, with the council and most offices open to all except the poorest citizens, the assembly and juries in the law courts open to all, and the balance of power between council and assembly such that the assembly met frequently and decided many matters with only slight limits on its freedom. By the middle of the century, the word *demokratia* ('people power') had been coined for such régimes, and *oligarchia* ('few rule') and *aristokratia* ('best power') for more restricted régimes, and Athens was self-consciously democratic and willing on occasions to encourage or impose democratic régimes in other member states of the Delian League. But to play a leading role in politics a man had to be rich enough not to need to work regularly for his living, and in the generation of Pericles the leading men tended still to come from the families which had provided leaders for the past century or more. On the Athenian democracy, see further Chapter 2.

Sparta was unusual among the Greek cities, with the citizens comprising a particularly small proportion of the total population. Though some Spartans were richer than others, they spent much of their time in communal living, and there was a measure of political equality among the citizens. However, there were two hereditary kings, who commanded the army and were life members of the *gerousia* ('council of elders'). The other members of the *gerousia* were men over sixty, elected for what remained of their life from a limited range of families. But to counterbalance these there were also five ephors ('overseers'), elected annually from all the citizens with no possibility of re-election, and they had considerable executive power and convened the *gerousia* and the assembly. The assembly met only to decide important matters; in it only the kings, ephors and other members of the *gerousia* could make speeches and put forward proposals, and probably the assembly's right to make the final decision mattered only when there was a division among them. Sparta was not a typical oligarchy, but it encouraged oligarchies among its allies.

The ideal member of a Greek citizen community was the farmer–soldier, who owned and farmed land and lived at least partly off the produce of it (commonly non-citizens could not own land in the city unless given a special dispensation to do so), and fought as a hoplite (heavy infantryman) in his city's army. Athens had developed further in a commercial direction than many cities, so a lower proportion of the citizens will have approximated to that ideal in Athens than elsewhere. Of agricultural products, Athens tended to export surplus olive oil and to import grain (particularly from the Black Sea and Egypt). At the other extreme, all full citizens of Sparta owned land and had helots to farm it, which gave them both the leisure and the need to devote themselves to military training. Slaves were widespread in the Greek world, but Sparta was unusual in having such a large body of indigenous slaves: Athens' slaves came from a variety of places, many being non-Greek, and they were mostly captured in war or purchased.

A city's population would also include free non-citizens, immigrants or descendants of immigrants from elsewhere (such men might be granted citizenship as a reward for conferring some benefit, but there was no right for immigrants to apply for citizenship). Since usually they could not own land, they particularly engaged in commercial and other activities which were not land based; in Athens, they were known as metics (migrants), and were fairly numerous. Athens before the Peloponnesian War had perhaps 60,000 adult male citizens, 240,000 citizens with their families. Numbers of other inhabitants are even harder to estimate, but in 431 there were at least 3,000 and perhaps 6,000 adult male metics rich enough to fight as hoplites (cf. Thuc. II. 13. vi–ix, 31. ii). Thucydides' claim that more than 20,000 slaves deserted in

and after 431 (Thuc. VII. 27. v) suggests that total slave numbers were in the tens of thousands rather than either the hundreds or the hundreds of thousands; probably there were somewhat more slaves, but not many times more, than there were adult male citizens and metics.

It was typical for a man aged about twenty-five to thirty to marry a woman aged about fifteen. It was assumed, though poor families were less likely than rich to be able to live up to the assumption, that there were separate roles for men and for women: men engaged in outdoor life (politics, farming, hunting, fighting) while women were responsible for the household and for giving birth to citizen children (but there was a role for them in public religious observances). Since infant mortality was common, families tended to have many children; and since property was divided among the children (in Athens, women inherited only in the absence of sons, to transmit the property to the men of the next generation), if too many children survived to adulthood, there was a risk of impoverishment from the division of the property into too many small shares.

Rich men were likely to own several separate plots of land rather than a single large estate; and, while in a small city many of the citizens would live in the town and go out by day to work in the fields, Athens and other large cities had a variety of villages and separate farmhouses in the countryside (cf. Thuc. II. 14, 16). For other economic activities, we should think of small-scale crafts rather than organized industry. Similarly long-distance trade depended on owners/captains of individual ships and other merchants who took a passage on them, not on commercial fleets. In fifth-century Athens, because of its command of the sea, goods from everywhere could be bought (Thuc. II. 38. ii, [Xen.] *Ath. Pol.* ii. 7); and, because of the many cash payments for civilian service and for rowing the navy's ships, Athens had more of a monetary economy than most cities, and many of the inhabitants were likely to handle coinage regularly. Athens in the time of Pericles erected grand public buildings, but complaints against rich men in the fourth century (Dem. XXIII. *Aristocrates* 206–9, III. *Olynthiac iii.* 25–6) suggest that in the fifth century even the rich lived in fairly modest houses.

Pericles and Athens

Particular topics are treated in the chapters which follow, but here I give an outline narrative which brings the topics together and indicates the various ways in which and occasions on which Pericles was involved.

Pericles was born about 498–494, into one of a group of intermarried families which provided many of the leading figures of sixth- and fifth-century Athens (see fig. 1.2). His family belonged to, and presumably lived in, the deme (local settlement) of Cholargus, perhaps 7 kilometres (4½ miles) north of the city centre. His mother Agariste was from the Alcmaeonid family, which had been prominent in Athenian politics since our information begins, in the second half of the seventh century. Her great-great-grandfather Megacles was archon (principal official) of Athens when in the 630s or 620s a man called Cylon tried to seize power as tyrant: the *coup* failed. Megacles was said to have promised to spare the lives of Cylon's supporters, but to have broken that promise; and as a result a curse was pronounced on the family, which was invoked against it on various occasions down to the late fifth century. Agariste was a niece of Cleisthenes, who was responsible for the reorganization of Athens' citizen body in 508/7, shortly after the ending of the tyranny of the Pisistratids, a reorganization which played an important part in the development of the democracy.

We do not know the background of Pericles' father, Xanthippus, but he successfully prosecuted Miltiades, the victor of the battle of Marathon in 490, for 'deceiving the people' when he tried but failed to capture the island of Paros afterwards. He was prominent enough to be one of the first men to be sent into exile by the procedure of ostracism, in 485/4. The Aristotelian *Athenian Constitution* describes him as the first victim of ostracism 'apart from the tyranny' (*Ath. Pol.* 22. vi), which in spite of his Alcmaeonid wife seems intended to distinguish him from the earliest victims, who were Pisistratids and Alcmaeonids suspected of disloyalty at the time of Marathon; but one man voted against Xanthippus by writing two lines of verse, whose meaning is ambiguous but may indicate that that voter did regard him

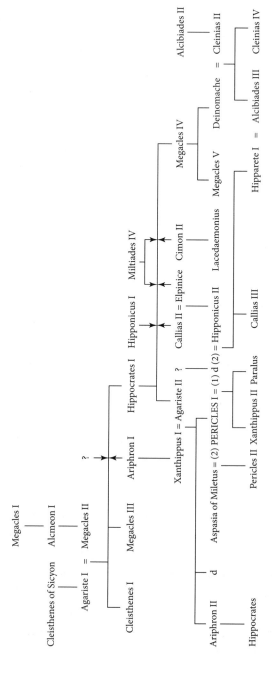

Figure 1.2 Pericles and his family.

This selective table shows Pericles and some of those related to him. Bearers of the same name are numbered as in J. K. Davies, *Athenian Propertied Families, 600–300 BC* (Oxford University Press, 1971); the Pericles who is central to this book is Pericles I.

as subject to the curse on the Alcmaeonids. When the men who had been ostracized were recalled at the time of the Persian invasion in 480, he returned, and was among the generals elected for 480/79 and 479/8 (by coincidence, another Xanthippus was archon in 479/8). In 479, he commanded the Athenian contingent in the Greek force which fought against the Persians at Mycale in Asia Minor; and when the Spartans returned home after that he commanded the remnant of the Greek force which captured Sestos in the Hellespont.

Pericles was the younger of two sons. Hardly anything is known about the elder, Ariphron. However, three *ostraka* survive which were used to vote against him in an ostracism in the 480s or 470s; and, fascinatingly, he and Pericles were two out of six drinkers who scratched their names on a cup found in a tomb at Cephisia (cf. fig. 1.3). He was still alive in the 430s, and he had a son, Hippocrates, who served as a general in the 420s and was killed at the battle of Delium in 424/3. There was also a daughter, about whom we know only that she died of the plague which first hit Athens in 430 (cf. p. 22). Herodotus (who probably finished writing his history in the 420s), in his only mention of Pericles, says in

Figure 1.3 *Skyphos* with the names of Aristides, Diodotus, Daesimus (?), Ariphron, Pericles and Eucritus.

an account of the Alcmaeonid family that, when Agariste was pregnant, she dreamed that she gave birth to a lion, and a few days later she did give birth to Pericles (Hdt. VI. 131. ii).

Plutarch has no stories about the young Pericles. We may assume that he had the normal upbringing of an upper-class Athenian boy: suckled by a wet nurse as an infant, and then entrusted to a *paidagogos* ('boy-leader') who would attend to him at home and take him to and from school. Physically, he had an elongated head, which was to provide opportunities for mockery by comic poets, and is said to explain why sculptors portrayed him in a military helmet (Plut. *Per.* 3. iii–vii: cf. fig. 1.4).

He will have been a boy of four to eight when the Persians first invaded and were defeated at Marathon, and ten to fourteen when his father was ostracized. We do not know where Xanthippus went during his exile, or whether he took his family with him or left them in Athens.

Figure 1.4 British Museum: Bust of Pericles.

Pericles will have been in his teens, but not yet quite adult and liable for military service, when the Persians returned to Greece in 480. The whole family certainly will have left Athens, as almost the whole of the population did, when the Persian forces arrived in Attica then; and it may well be that their house was destroyed. Women and children went to Aegina, in the Saronic Gulf, and to Troezen, in the Argolid. When they returned, after the final defeat of the Persians in 479, the city walls were rebuilt as a matter of urgency, and essential public buildings will have been rebuilt; temples which the Persians had destroyed were at first left in ruins (cf. pp. 81–2); families will have had to repair or rebuild their houses and resume their livelihoods.

Pericles will have been admitted to membership of Xanthippus' phratry ('brotherhood', a group claiming descent from an ancestor in the mythical past) at the age of sixteen and membership of the deme of Cholargus (the procedure by which he was formally acknowledged as an adult citizen) at eighteen. There may already in this period have been some possibilities of military training for young citizens, but we know no details earlier than a major overhaul of the system in the 330s. We hear no more of Xanthippus after the military campaign of 479, and it is likely that he died within the next few years. The first dated reference to Pericles is that he served as *choregos*, the rich citizen who was appointed to the 'liturgy' of financing the production of a set of plays at a festival (cf. ch. 2), for the tragedian Aeschylus in 473/2 (*IG* ii² 2318. 9–11), and this implies that by then Xanthippus was dead and Pericles was master of his own property. At this date he will have been under thirty, so not yet eligible to hold any offices, but serving as *choregos* enabled him to attract attention.

What is known of Pericles' sons suggests that he was married by *c.* 460 at the latest. In his funeral oration of 431/0, Pericles is represented by Thucydides as saying of 'the virtues of a wife' that there should be 'the least possible talk of you among men either for praise or for blame' (Thuc. II. 45. ii). What that tells us about the position of women in fifth-century Athens is endlessly debated, but it is striking that, just as we do not know the name of Pericles' sister, we do not know the name or the family of his wife; Plutarch says that she was related to him (Plut. *Per.* 24. viii), but we do not know the basis for that, and have no other information.

By the time of Pericles' service as *choregos*, Athens had become the leader of the Delian League, the alliance formed to continue fighting against Persia, and was already finding ways of using the League to its own advantage (for instance, by occupying Scyros, an island in the northern Aegean which lay on the route between Athens and the Hellespont). Regularly serving as commander of the League's forces was Cimon, son of the Miltiades of the battle of Marathon, who believed in remaining on good terms with Sparta (he gave the name Lacedaemonius, 'Spartan', to one of his sons, and he is said to have been uncultured in the Spartan manner) and who in that respect and in others was opposed to Themistocles, who after 480–479 saw Sparta as a rival to Athens. About the late 470s, the procedure of ostracism removed Themistocles from Athens and left Cimon without his principal opponent. (Diodorus Siculus, writing in the first century BC a universal history in which material was presented year by year, in XI. 54–9 gives the whole story of Themistocles' downfall under the year 471/0, but we cannot be confident that that was the year of the ostracism or of any other particular event in the story.)

One of the plays of Aeschylus which Pericles financed was *Persians*, unique among surviving tragedies in dealing with an event from the recent past, the Persians' reaction to their defeat by the Greeks in 480. It focuses on the battle of Salamis, and (though without naming him) on the trick by which Themistocles was said to have induced the Persians to fight against the Greeks there. In the circumstances of the late 470s, that looks like championing of Themistocles at a time when he was under attack; and a few years later, when after a great success Cimon and his fellow generals were asked to act as judges of the tragic competition, they awarded the prize not to Aeschylus but to the young Sophocles (Plut. *Cim.* 8. vii–ix). On Athenian drama, and also art and architecture, see further Chapter 5.

And Pericles is next attested in conflict with Cimon. From 465/4 to 463/2, Cimon commanded against the northern Aegean island of

Thasos, when it tried to secede from the Delian League; and in his *euthynai*, the accounting process which all office holders were required to undergo, he was accused of taking bribes to spare Macedon. Unusually for Athens, prosecution was not left to volunteers, but public prosecutors were appointed, and Pericles was one of them. It was alleged that Cimon's sister Elpinice tried to win over Pericles, and that consequently Pericles was very gentle in presenting his case (e.g. Plut. *Per.* 10. vi). We may accept that Cimon was acquitted; how much substance, if any, there was to the allegation, we cannot say.

Plutarch paints a picture of Pericles' political development: at first he followed a military career and avoided politics; after a time he entered politics on the popular side, in opposition to the aristocratic Cimon; and eventually he became a kingly leader (Plut. *Per.* 7–9, 15–16). The change from democratic politician to kingly leader seems to be a result of Plutarch's trying to reconcile different pictures of Pericles given by different sources; the early avoidance of politics may be an inference from the fact that no involvement of his in politics (or indeed in fighting) is recorded until he was over thirty. What probably can be accepted is the depiction of Pericles as aloof rather than populist in manner, avoiding social occasions and addressing the assembly occasionally and with care rather than again and again (Plut. *Per.* 5. iii, 7. v–8). Pericles left no speeches or other writings of his own, but he had a reputation as an able speaker (his opponent Thucydides is said to have complained that whenever he threw down Pericles in wrestling, Pericles could persuade people that he had not been thrown down: Plut. *Per.* 8. v). Some writers quote what they claim to be striking phrases from his speeches. Aristotle says that in his funeral oration (perhaps an oration delivered in connection with the Samian war of 440–439) Pericles stated that the youth had been removed from the city as if the spring had been taken out of the year (Arist. *Rhet.* I. 1365 A 31–3); and Plutarch says that a few sayings of his were recorded, for instance his instruction to eliminate Aegina (the island state in the middle of the Saronic Gulf) as the eyesore of the Piraeus (Plut. *Per.* 8. vii–ix). He is said also to have been uninterested in the land which he owned, selling all the produce and then buying what he needed in the market, and to the annoyance of his family living not extravagantly but within his means (Plut. *Per.* 16. iii–vi, 36. i–iv).

Pericles is next linked with a series of events in which internal and external politics were interwoven. A serious earthquake which hit Sparta *c.* 464/3 prompted a revolt by the non-citizen population, particularly the helots living in Messenia. Sparta asked for help from allies, including Athens: Cimon wanted to help, but other Athenians including a man called Ephialtes did not. However, Cimon got his way and took an army to Messenia. In Cimon's absence, in 462/1, Ephialtes carried through the assembly a reform which took from the council of the Areopagus (to which men who had held office as archons belonged for the remainder of their lives) judicial powers of political significance, and which can be seen as asserting the democratic nature of Athens. The Spartans, perhaps afraid that the Athenian army might be given new instructions, to support the rebels, reacted by dismissing Cimon and his army. Cimon on his return tried without success to overturn the reform, and was ostracized – for being pro-Spartan and anti-democratic – while Athens broke off its alliance with Sparta and made alliances with enemies of Sparta (external dimension Thuc. I. 102; internal dimension *Ath. Pol.* 25; both Plut. *Cim.* 15. i–17. iii, *Per.* 9. iii–v). Plutarch mentions Pericles as involved with Ephialtes in the reform; *Ath. Pol.*, perhaps through trying to reconcile different sources, does not associate them in that way but has a later reform of the Areopagus by Pericles (*Ath. Pol.* 27. i). Ephialtes was assassinated not long afterwards, and from then onwards Pericles was a leading figure in Athenian public life.

Internally, in the years after 462/1, there were further constitutional developments: the opening of the office of archon to citizens of middling wealth, the establishment of travelling justices to try lesser lawsuits locally; also (both attributed to Pericles) a law requiring an Athenian mother as well as an Athenian father to qualify for citizenship, and, as the first of a series of such stipends, payment for serving on the juries of the increasingly busy law courts.

Externally, Athens at the head of the Delian League continued to fight against Persia, in the 450s particularly but in the end unsuccessfully in Egypt, where a rebel against Persia had asked for Athenian support. But now it also set about challenging Sparta's predominant position on the Greek mainland. The First Peloponnesian War began *c.* 460 when Megara, on the Isthmus of Corinth and involved in a dispute with Corinth, defected from the Peloponnesians and joined Athens; and within the next few years Athens gained the island of Aegina, and Boeotia and other parts of central Greece. The first military episode in which Pericles is known to have been involved was a campaign in the Gulf of Corinth, *c.* 454. To make a single fortified area of Athens and its harbour town of Piraeus, long walls were built linking Athens and Piraeus: two walls in the 450s and a third wall, between the first two, perhaps in the 440s and on the proposal of Pericles.

Athens' expansion ran out of steam; and in 451, perhaps after the return of Cimon from ostracism and with his help, a five-year truce was made between Athens and the Peloponnesians. Soon after that Cimon was killed on a campaign in Cyprus. Persia had perhaps attempted a recovery in the Aegean after Athens' failure in Egypt, but after Cimon's death regular fighting against Persia came to an end. Later texts contrast the glories of the Peace of Callias, thought to have marked Athens' final success against Persia, with the humiliation of the King's Peace of 387/6, which returned the Greek cities of Asia Minor to Persia and established Persia as the underwriter of a settlement among the Greeks, but I hold to the minority view that the treaty was invented after 387/6 to make more real the contrast between the glory of the past and the disgrace of the present.

The League was kept in being (an attempt attributed to Pericles, to refashion it as a league of all the Greeks, came to nothing when Sparta declined Athens' invitation), and the monetary tribute now paid by nearly all the member states continued to be collected. After a generation in which temples destroyed by the Persians had been left in ruins, in 447/6 Athens began to set up buildings on the acropolis – including the Parthenon, a new kind of national temple of Athena – and elsewhere.

These were public buildings, erected at public expense under the supervision of publicly appointed boards; and Athenians subsequently regarded these both as dedications for victory over the Persians and as works of Pericles. Possibly directly and certainly indirectly, the tribute from the League helped to pay for these buildings. This became the principal ground for complaint against Pericles by Thucydides, son of Melesias, a relative of Cimon, who became Pericles' leading opponent after Cimon's death; but Pericles received the backing of the assembly, and eventually, *c*. 444/<u>3</u>, Thucydides was ostracized (Plut. *Per*. 11–14: cf. chs. 2, 3, 5).

In the Delian League, Athens encountered trouble in various places and reacted firmly, and it impinged on the member states in a growing range of ways. In 447/6 rebellions began close to Athens. Boeotia revolted after about ten years of Athenian control, and defeated an Athenian army and succeeded in asserting its independence. Then the cities of the island of Euboea revolted; while Pericles was there, Megara defected and Sparta led a Peloponnesian invasion of Attica. Pericles returned to Athens; the Peloponnesians withdrew, and it was believed that Pericles had bribed them. Perhaps he had in fact undertaken that Athens would agree to the terms which it subsequently did agree to. He went back to Euboea and restored Athenian control there, but in 446/5 Athens made the Thirty Years' Peace with Sparta, by which it gave up the territories which it had gained on the mainland. This seemed to represent a victory for Sparta, but it became apparent that Athens was still eager to expand outside Sparta's area of influence, and in the years which followed Athens was involved in settlements and made alliances from Sicily and southern Italy to the Black Sea and Crimea. Perhaps in the mid-430s, Pericles himself led an expedition to the Black Sea and founded a colony at Sinope on its south coast.

From the ages of the children it seems to have been about 455 that Pericles divorced his wife, giving her to Hipponicus (whose mother was Cimon's sister Elpinice; Plut. *Per*. 24. viii makes Hipponicus not her second husband but her first). Scandalmongers accused him of various kinds of (hetero)sexual misconduct (Plut. *Per*. 13. xv–xvi), whether with some justification or simply in reaction against his austere public image. Some time in the 440s he took as consort Aspasia of Miletus. She bore him a son, another Pericles, who under Pericles' citizenship law of 451/0 could not be an Athenian citizen; but after his two sons by his Athenian wife had both died from the plague the younger Pericles was made a citizen. Pericles was notoriously a father who did not manage to bring up his sons to match himself (e.g. Pl. *Meno* 93 A–94 E); he also, after the death of their father in 447/6, became guardian of his distant relatives Alcibiades (who was to be a maverick politician in the last decades of the century) and Cleinias.

Aspasia had intellectual interests, and Pericles associated with some of the leading intellectuals of the time. One was the Athenian Damon, a contemporary of his: he was particularly interested in music and its emotional effects; he was a friend of Pericles and was said to have been a political adviser of his (in particular, he was said to have suggested the introduction of jury pay); and he was ostracized, probably in the late 440s. Another was Anaxagoras of Clazomenae, also a contemporary, who arrived in Athens perhaps in 456/5. He was interested in natural phenomena and physical explanations of them; Plutarch has a story of his cutting open the skull of a one-horned ram to show that it was not portentous but had a natural cause (Plut. *Per.* 4. vi–6). Pericles was closely involved also with the sculptor Pheidias, whom Plutarch believed, but perhaps mistakenly, to have had general responsibility for the building programme on the acropolis in the 440s and 430s.

There were attacks in the 430s on Pericles and on people connected with him: Pheidias was accused of embezzlement after completing his statue of Athena for the Parthenon in 438/7; Aspasia was prosecuted or perhaps simply attacked in a comedy for impiety; a decree making it an offence 'not to believe in divine things or to teach about things up in the air' may have served as a basis for a prosecution of Anaxagoras, perhaps by the demagogue Cleon. Pericles himself was prosecuted, perhaps in connection with the charge against Pheidias, and presumably was acquitted (Plut. *Per.* 31. ii–32, but linking these attacks with the outbreak of the Peloponnesian War in 431). A sign of sensitivity at this time is a decree 'concerning not comedying', enacted in 440/39 and annulled in 437/6 (schol. Ar. *Ach.* 67 ~ Fornara 111).

In 440–439 Athens supported Miletus when it was at war against Samos (Pericles was one of Athens' commanders, and it was alleged that he had been influenced by Aspasia). Samos was one of the few Delian League members which did not pay tribute but still contributed its own ships; it had support from Persia, and the Corinthians claimed that Sparta had wanted the Peloponnesian League to give its support but they had prevented that. This was a serious challenge to Athens, but Samos was eventually defeated.

Thucydides begins his account of the events leading to the Peloponnesian War with a dispute between Corinth and Corcyra, a large island state off the west coast of northern Greece which had been colonized by Corinth long before. In 433 Corcyra asked Athens for an alliance, Corinth argued against, and Athens made a purely defensive alliance with Corcyra and did have to use its forces to save Corcyra from defeat by Corinth. Athens' decision was close: Thucydides does not name Pericles or any other Athenian, but Plutarch thought, surely correctly, that Pericles did favour supporting Corcyra. The fact that one of the Athenian generals sent was Cimon's son Lacedaemonius suggests that the other side was strong enough to have one of its own men appointed (Thuc. I. 24–55; Plut. *Per.* 29. i–iii, but with a different explanation of Lacedaemonius' appointment). About the same time, Athens wound up the acropolis building programme and put its sacred funds (on which it would draw to finance the war) in order; and, expecting a war in which the west would be involved, it reaffirmed alliances made earlier with Rhegium on the toe of Italy and Leontini in Sicily.

Next Athens put pressure on Potidaea, in the north-west of the Aegean, a colony of Corinth but a member of the Delian League, and there was again fighting between Athens and Corinth (Thuc. I. 56–66). Corinth led member states of the Peloponnesian League in putting pressure on Sparta; further grievances against Athens arose from Megara and Aegina, and Thucydides gives a speech by Athenians in Sparta which is unapologetic about Athenian power and warns the

Spartans not to go to war against Athens lightly. Sparta decided to go to war unless Athens backed down; and Thucydides thought that Sparta was persuaded by its fear of Athenian power rather than by the particular complaints (Thuc. I. 67–88).

During the winter of 432/1, the Spartans tried to invoke the curse on the Alcmaeonid family, from the seventh century (cf. above), against Pericles, and the Athenians responded with Spartan curses. They then urged Athens to give way on the particular complaints, especially Megara's complaint about the economic sanctions to which it was being subjected by Athens, and more fundamentally to allow the Greeks their freedom (Thuc. I. 119–39). Thucydides had already said of Pericles that 'in leading the state he was totally opposed to the Spartans, and would not allow the Athenians to give way but impelled them towards the war' (Thuc. I. 127. iii), and he ended Book I with a speech in which Pericles argued that if there had to be war Athens should accept it and was ready for it (Thuc. I. 140–5). I believe that Athens' actions after 446/5 showed it still to be too ambitious for Sparta's comfort, and that as the war approached the Athenians, and Pericles in particular, were not willing to back down but thought that if war had to come it should come when they could claim to be technically in the right and when they were better prepared than their opponents. Plutarch records the claim attributed to Pericles, 'None of the citizens put on a black cloak [as a sign of mourning] because of me' (Plut. *Per.* 38. iv) – but if he did make that claim he was excluding deaths in warfare from the reckoning.

War came in 431. After a pre-emptive strike by Thebes on Athens' Boeotian ally Plataea, Sparta's king Archidamus with a Peloponnesian army formally invaded Attica. The Spartans expected the Athenians to go out of the city to fight them, and were confident that they could defeat the Athenians. But Pericles urged the Athenians to abandon the countryside, stay inside their fortifications, and rely on their superior sea power to import what they needed from abroad and to make counter-raids on the Peloponnese; with their ample financial resources they could outlast the Peloponnesians. Thucydides perhaps oversimplifies. In 431 and 430 the Athenians made very large-scale raids on the Peloponnese, and an inscription shows that in the first two or three years of the war they were using up their money at a rate which would not have allowed them to keep going for long. I suspect that Pericles was cautious in his public pronouncements and that Thucydides reflects them, but privately he hoped, mistakenly, that after a few years of making no headway against Athens the Peloponnesians would admit that they could not win.

In 431 some Athenians wanted to go out and fight against the invaders (Thuc. II. 21–2). In the following winter, Pericles was appointed to give the funeral oration for those who had been killed in the first year's fighting (in fact, not very many or very heroically): in the speech which Thucydides attributes to him he concentrated on the achievements of Athens' democratic society and its empire in recent decades, as what they were fighting to preserve, and stressed the need for individual citizens to be 'lovers' of the city (Thuc. II. 36–46).

In 430, owing partly to the crowding of the citizens inside the fortified area, Athens was hit by a plague, which continued until 426/5; about a third of the population was killed by it. Thucydides was among those who suffered from it, and has given a detailed account (Thuc. II. 47. iii–54, III. 87). Pericles also suffered from it, and died in the autumn of 429; his sister, and both of his sons by his Athenian wife, died from it (Plut. *Per.* 36. vi–ix, 38. i–ii). When the Peloponnesians invaded again that year, the Athenians' morale was weakened. Envoys were sent to Sparta who tried without success to make peace. Thucydides gives Pericles another speech, in defence of his policies; but he was fined and deposed from his generalship. After a change of mood he was re-elected for the following year, but Thucydides does not mention, and we do not know of, anything that he said or did between then and his death (Thuc. II. 59–65. iv).

Except in one cross reference, Pericles does not appear again in Thucydides' text, but he is ushered off the stage at this point, with a premature but glowing obituary notice. According to Thucydides, he was an outstandingly able and an incorruptible leader, and one who led the people rather than let them lead him, so that 'the result was in theory democracy but in fact rule by the first man'. Athens had reached its greatest height under his leadership, and his policy for the war would have brought success, but subsequent politicians competed in pandering to the people, and Athens might still not have been defeated if it had not been torn by internal disputes (Thuc. II. 65. v–xiii).

Thucydides the historian, related to Pericles' opponents Cimon and Thucydides, son of Melesias, strongly approved of Pericles, but had broken from his family tradition in doing so, and some of his opinions are open to question. No man could in fact have been so powerful within Athens' democratic structure as Thucydides represents Pericles as being, and his deposition in 430 reminds us of that. There is evidence which indicates that Pericles was never an unchallenged leader, but had opponents of various kinds and on various grounds throughout his career (cf. ch. 2). His strategy for the war can be questioned too. The defensive strategy which Thucydides believed in might have avoided defeat but it would not have brought victory. I suggested above that Pericles perhaps thought that after a short time the Peloponnesians would acknowledge that they could not win, but the strategy actually followed while Pericles was alive used up Athens' financial reserves rapidly and would not have allowed Athens to outlast the Peloponnesians in a long war. After his death more adventurous strategies were attempted, sometimes with success and sometimes not (cf. ch. 6). The Sicilian campaign of 415–413 was a major turning point, as Thucydides recognized (Thuc. II. 65. xi). Even after it, there were times when it seemed that Athens might win; but in the end Persian backing enabled the Peloponnesians to persevere until Athens could no longer do so.

However, it remains true that in the middle of the fifth century Athens did reach great heights – of democracy, of power in the Greek world, of prosperity and of cultural achievement in various fields – and that Pericles, though never supremely powerful, was for much of that time predominant and associated with much that the Athenians did.

2

Democracy

Development

The democracy of Periclean Athens was the result of a long development, of a kind which has parallels in other Greek cities but which Athens had taken further than most. From what point the word 'democracy' should be used of it is debated, but recognition of the process is more important than deciding on a right answer to that question. The earliest evidence for what became the Greeks' standard threefold categorization of *monarchia* (single-person rule), *oligarchia* (few rule) and *demokratia* (people power) – if we assume that the debate which Herodotus sets in Persia in 522 (Hdt. III. 80–2) belongs not there but to Greece in his own time – is in a poem of Pindar perhaps to be dated 468 (Pind. *Pyth.* ii. 86–8). Aeschylus' *Suppliant Women*, probably of 464/3, is very insistent on democratic procedure in Argos of the legendary period, and at one point seems to reflect the word *demokratia* in referring to a vote by the 'ruling hand of the people', *demou kratousa cheir* (Aesch. *Supp.* 600–5: voting by show of hands was a regular Greek practice). I therefore believe that the distinction within constitutional government between democracy and oligarchy, and the words used to mark that distinction, first appeared about the 470s–460s, and I shall suggest below that the reform of Ephialtes in 462/1 was the first constitutional change made in Athens with an explicitly democratic intention.

The earliest attested event in Athenian history was the attempt by Cylon to seize power as 'tyrant' (a ruler outside the city's normal structures), in the 630s or 620s. The people backed the authorities against him, and the attempt failed; it was said that his supporters had been promised that their lives would be spared, but the promise was broken, and the blame fell on Megacles (Megacles I in fig 1.2 on p. 10), who was the one of Athens' nine archons ('rulers', the annually appointed senior officials of the city) entitled simply 'archon'. This had various repercussions, including the pronouncing of a curse on Megacles and his whole family, the curse which the Spartans tried to invoke against Pericles before the outbreak of the Peloponnesian War. Probably to be connected with the aftermath of this episode also was the compilation of Athens' first written laws, including laws on homicide, by Draco in 621/0.

Although there had not been enough discontent to carry Cylon to power, the discontent increased, until in 594/3 Solon as archon was given a special commission to mediate between the advantaged and disadvantaged. Economically, he liberated a class of dependent peasants, making them the absolute owners of the land which they farmed, and banned the enslavement of defaulting debtors. Politically, he made the membership of one of four economic classes the sole qualification for office-holding (thus admitting to offices members of families which had become rich but were until then excluded from them), and he strengthened the position of the citizens' assembly by creating a new council of four hundred members to prepare its business, separate from the already-existing council of the Areopagus (which consisted of former archons and would therefore continue to be dominated by the old ruling families for some time). He also compiled a new code of laws, superseding whatever laws Draco had produced in areas other than homicide, and improved people's chances of obtaining justice by providing for appeals to a court against the verdicts of individual officials and by creating a category of 'public' lawsuits in which prosecution was not limited to the injured parties and their families but could be undertaken by any citizen. This was not yet democracy – Solon wrote of the people's 'following their leaders' (Solon fr. 6 West *ap. Ath. Pol.* 12. ii) – but it was a basis on which democracy could be built.

Neither side was satisfied, and later in the sixth century Athens did experience tyranny. After two short-lived periods of power, *c.* 561 and *c.* 556, Pisistratus succeeded in making himself tyrant in 546/5; and when he died in 528/7 he was followed by his eldest sons, Hippias and Hipparchus. He is said to have been a benign ruler, working through existing institutions rather than overriding them. Tyranny was in general detrimental to the members of the upper class, since they no less than the other citizens were subject to one man or family; but at any rate by the 520s some of the leading families were acquiescing in the régime. We happen to know from an inscription that Cleisthenes, great-grandson of the Megacles who had had Cylon's supporters killed, and uncle of Pericles' mother Agariste, was archon in 525/4 (M&L 6. *c.* 3 = *IG* i³ 1031. 18 ~ Fornara 23. C. 3).

But opposition to the Pisistratids developed. Hipparchus was assassinated in 514. Cleisthenes' family, the Alcmaeonids, used its influence at Delphi to put pressure on Sparta, and in 511/0 a force from Sparta expelled Hippias. Rivalry then followed between Cleisthenes and another prominent man, Isagoras, and Isagoras was elected archon for 508/7. Next, Cleisthenes put forward proposals for a new organization of the citizen body which would complement the political structures of the city with structures in the separate local communities. Now Isagoras called in the Spartans, perhaps fearing or claiming to fear that Cleisthenes would become another tyrant; but the people backed Cleisthenes against Isagoras and the Spartans, Isagoras departed into exile and Cleisthenes brought his new organization into effect.

In the new system, 139 local settlements, including five inside the town, were given an institutional existence as demes (a special use of the word *demos* = 'people'), with their own assemblies and officials. These were grouped in three regions: 'city', comprising the town of Athens and most of the plain around it; 'coast', comprising all the coastal territory apart from that included in the city region; and 'inland'. Ten new 'tribes' were created, and each tribe consisted of three groups of demes called *trittyes* ('thirds'), one from each of the three regions. This new system became the basis of Athens' public life. Solon's council of four hundred became a council of five hundred, with fifty members from each tribe, and within the tribal contingents representatives of the individual demes in proportion to their size. Many other appointments were based on the tribes, with frequent use of boards of ten men (or occasionally five or a multiple of ten). The army was organized in tribal regiments. Some of the *trittyes* were geographically compact, but others were not. From what we know of the details of this system, Cleisthenes seems to have been trying to break old local groupings through which established families had been able to exert influence (his own family was not well placed in that respect), and at the same time to give his own family a good position in the new system, with its country estates to the south-east of the town assigned to the same tribes as its homes in and near the town.

Several words incorporating *iso-* ('equal', or 'fair') were applied to Athens after its liberation from the tyranny and to this dispensation in Athens, and we may assume that Cleisthenes' claim was that by 'mixing the people up' in this way he was making Athens a fairer city, in which 'more men could have a share in political power' (*Ath. Pol.* 21. ii); but the advantage for his own family built into the details suggests that like Solon he still expected the people to follow their leaders. However, Cleisthenes' new system, with constitutional machinery at local level and intermediate levels as well as at city level, required a large number of men willing to attend meetings and hold offices. If that had not occurred, the system would have broken down; but it did occur; and so, whether Cleisthenes had intended or foreseen it or not, over the next half century a large number of Athenians gained experience in and a taste for political activity.

One product of Cleisthenes' organization was the election by the assembly each year of ten *strategoi* ('generals'), one from each tribe, as commanders not simply of their tribal regiments but of the army as a whole, which had previously been the responsibility of the one among the nine archons entitled polemarch ('war-archon'). The generals were elected and could be re-elected, whereas a man could be archon only once, and in 487/6 an element of allotment was introduced for the appointment of archons (probably that had been introduced earlier, by Solon, but Pisistratus had reverted to direct election). The fifth century was the period of Athens' greatest military (and naval) success, and by the time of Pericles the generalship rather than the archonship was the office which attracted ambitious men, so in effect in that period the Athenians elected their political leaders. Not later than 441/0, while the rule of one general per tribe remained the norm, exceptions were made possible (for instance, two from one tribe and none from one other). What seems the best explanation is a recognition that there might be times when one tribe had no suitable candidate, and on such occasions it was perhaps made possible for such a tribe to adopt a member of another tribe as its candidate.

Cleisthenes also introduced the procedure of ostracism (named after the *ostrakon*, potsherd, on which each voter wrote the name of the man he was voting against: several thousands of these have survived; cf. fig. 2.1), by which each year the people had the opportunity to send one man into a kind of honourable exile for ten years. If the assembly decided to hold an ostracism, there was a special voting session, at which there was no list of candidates but each citizen was free to vote against his preferred victim; and as long as there were at least 6,000 votes in all the man with the largest number was ostracized. Some men

Figure 2.1 *Ostraka* used for voting against Aristides, Themistocles, Cimon and Pericles.

doubtless voted against a personal enemy, but those who attracted large numbers of votes were presumably voted against as public figures. When introduced, ostracism may have been represented as a means to prevent the rise of another tyrant, but it was not in fact suitable for that purpose, since a potential tyrant might be able to ensure that another man received more votes than he did. It was first used in the years after the battle of Marathon, against men with Pisistratid and Alcmaeonid connections who were suspected of disloyalty then but who to be ostracized did not have to be judged guilty in a law court (among them was Megacles, a brother of Pericles' mother Agariste); but afterwards it seems to have been used as a safety valve to choose between rival political leaders, by removing the 'loser' for ten years and allowing the 'winner' a clear run. Thus in the later 480s, in what I see as a three-cornered rivalry, Aristides and Pericles' father Xanthippus were ostracized but Themistocles was not.

Also in the later 480s, Athens spent the profits from its silver mines on enlarging its navy, to 200 triremes; and this navy enabled Athens to play a large part in resisting the Persians in 480–479, and in fighting Persia and building up its own power through the Delian League afterwards (cf. ch. 3). It had become normal in Greek cities for men rich enough to equip themselves and fight as 'hoplites' (heavy infantry) to see themselves as important to their city and to receive a share in political power. In Athens, the role of the navy gave comparable importance also to the poorer citizens, who rowed the ships, and this helps to explain the development of Athens' democracy in the fifth century.

After the Persian Wars, Themistocles appears in various stories which suggest that he saw Sparta as a rival to Athens, and Aristides organized the Delian League; but then Aristides disappeared from prominence, and Themistocles was ostracized in the late 470s and eventually became an exile among the Persians, while the pro-Spartan Cimon was commander of all the early campaigns of the League which we know of. By the 460s the notion of democracy, as power for the people at large rather than a privileged few, had become current. A survival from the older Athens was the powerful council of the Areopagus, recruited from the former archons who were no longer the leading men of the city, and Ephialtes, after prosecutions of individual members, in 462/1 (while Cimon was away supporting Sparta against the rebelling Messenians: see the narrative in ch. 1), persuaded the assembly to take from the Areopagus judicial powers which were of political importance, probably the procedures for controlling officials and the trial by *eisangelia* (often translated 'impeachment') of men accused of major offences against the state (*Ath. Pol.* 25. i–ii). There is a story (which is in fact chronologically impossible) that Themistocles was involved with Ephialtes in this; and Pericles does seem to have been one of Ephialtes' supporters (*Ath. Pol.* 25. iii–iv). Aeschylus, who had employed the idea of democracy in his *Suppliant Women*, in his *Eumenides* of 459/8 focused on the Areopagus as a homicide court, the role which it retained after Ephialtes, but in such a way that scholars continue to debate whether he approved or disapproved of the reform.

In the years after 462/1 there were further constitutional developments. From 457/6 the nine positions of archon, hitherto restricted to the two highest of the four property classes, were opened to the third also, which confirmed the new status of the archonship as a routine office rather than the principal office of state. In 453/2 travelling justices were instituted, to try lesser cases locally (such justices had been used earlier, under the Pisistratid tyranny, but presumably were abolished at the end of the tyranny; and probably after Ephialtes' reform the law courts were acquiring more business, and this was intended to relieve the pressure on them). In 451/0 a law of Pericles required an Athenian mother as well as an Athenian father as a qualification for citizenship, so that the benefits of being an Athenian citizen should be enjoyed only by those who were truly Athenian (*Ath. Pol.* 26. ii–iv). Also attributed to Pericles, not securely dated but probably in the 450s, was the institution of payment for serving on the juries of the increasingly busy law courts (*Ath. Pol.* 27. iii–iv, where 'Damonides' as Pericles' adviser is an error for 'Damon son of Damonides'). In *Ath. Pol.*'s hostile account, this was a device for bribing the people with public money, since Pericles was not rich enough to match Cimon in bribing the people with his own money: more charitably, it reflects a belief that the richest men ought not to be able to buy influence. This was the first of a series of such stipends for civilian service, which made it possible for citizens who needed to work for their living to exercise their political rights (but payment for attending the assembly was not introduced until *c.* 400). By this time, Athens was self-consciously democratic, and in a decree probably of the late 450s it imposed a democratic kind of constitution on Erythrae, a Delian League member in Asia Minor (*IG* i³ 14 = O&R 121 ~ Fornara 71: cf. ch. 3).

Formal mechanisms

Athens' ultimate decision-making body was the assembly, open to all citizens and regularly attended by several thousand of them. Some subsidiary matters were decided by the council of five hundred, but most decisions, on a range of subjects (from peace and war to religion, public appointments, buildings and so on), were made by the assembly. Its business was prepared by the council, and within the council each tribal contingent of fifty served as the 'prytany', the standing committee, for a tenth of the year. Probably by 431, the assembly had forty regular meetings a year, four in each prytany, and could have additional meetings when needed. The council met every day apart from about sixty days excluded for religious reasons. The council drew up the agenda for the assembly, with some business prescribed for particular occasions, and the assembly could not make a decision except on a matter placed on the agenda. But in Athens the council's control did not go further than that. On some matters it made a recommendation to the assembly, but on others it simply invited the assembly to decide; whether it made a recommendation or not, any citizen in the assembly could make a speech, and any citizen could propose an alternative motion or an amendment to a motion already under discussion. Decisions were made by a simple majority: the assembly voted by show of hands, and probably there was not a precise count (by the members of the prytany), but it was hoped that it would be clear which side had the larger vote.

There were no political parties, with members and programmes. There was a small number of leading politicians, who made speeches and put forward proposals frequently, but there seem also to have been many more men who made speeches and put forward proposals occasionally, perhaps on a subject in which they had a special interest or in a year in which they were serving in the council. Leading politicians will have had some men who supported them with various degrees of loyalty and for various reasons (including both personal connections and approval of the line they took on important issues), but there will always have been a significant number who went to a debate intending to decide on the basis of the arguments. Thucydides wrote of the predominance of Pericles as 'rule by the first man' (Thuc. II. 65. ix), but in fact the assembly was not entirely consistent in its decisions, and nobody could count on it to vote as he wanted again and again, or on any particular occasion.

While decision-making was done by all the citizens (or as many as attended) together in the assembly, administration, that is, implementing decisions, was done by many of the citizens in turn. There were no civil servants employed as permanent administrators (but there were a few state-owned slaves with clerkly jobs). The work was distributed among many officials or boards of officials, and most appointments were made for one year and could not be held by the same man more than once (though a man with a taste for it could hold different positions in different years). While an Athenian became adult and could attend the assembly at eighteen, to hold offices he had to be thirty. In the fifth century, members of the lowest property class were excluded from office-holding. Nearly all civilian appointments were made by lot, but military offices (where it was more important that each of the men appointed should command trust) were filled by election, and to them men could be reappointed. The council of five hundred also was appointed by lot, with numbers of seats assigned to demes: in the fourth century, a man could serve there twice in his life, but with

Athens' larger population before the Peloponnesian War repetition may then not have been allowed at all.

All Greek states considered it important that there should be a rotation of officials to prevent the development of a ruling clique, and that officials should be accountable to the qualified citizens (however those were defined). In Athens officials had to undergo a vetting process (*dokimasia*) before entering office, to check their general suitability as good citizens rather than their particular suitability for particular duties, and a financial accounting (*logos*) and a general examination (*euthynai*, 'straightening') on leaving office; and there were opportunities to check their conduct during the year too.

Taxing income was not feasible in a society in which most people did not earn regular wages. Most taxes were indirect, for instance on imports, and they were collected not by a government department but by 'tax farmers', groups of men who had bid for the right to collect a particular tax in a particular year. They were committed to paying to the state the amount which they had bid; if they had a surplus, that was their legitimate profit, but if there was a shortfall, they had to provide the remainder. A further means of obtaining money from the rich, and at the same time of channelling their ambitions in a useful direction, was the system of 'liturgies' (literally, 'public works'), by which a rich citizen was given a job to do at his own expense, most often by taking responsibility for a group of performers at a festival (and perhaps sometimes himself acting as leader of the performers) or taking charge of one of the navy's triremes for a year. Thus Pericles was the *choregos* (literally, 'chorus-leader') responsible for Aeschylus' tragedies in 473/2 (cf. ch. 1). Ambitious men might spend more money on a liturgy than the minimum which was needed, and might voluntarily perform more liturgies than were legally required of them; and in speeches in the law courts they often cited their liturgies as proof of their public-spiritedness. The possibility of an ad hoc tax on the property of the rich (*eisphora*, 'paying in') is first mentioned in an inscription of probably 434/3 (*IG* i³ 52 = O&R 144 ~ Fornara 119, *B*. 15–19), and there was such a levy in 428/7 (Thuc. III. 19. i). In the time of the Delian League, the tribute paid by the member states at least subsidized Athens by paying for military activity, and Athens may have found other ways of benefiting from the tribute too (cf. ch. 3).

Athens' participatory system was not the most efficient way to administer what by Greek standards was an unusually complex state, but the principle was that the work should be shared out among the good citizens rather than that it should be done by those best able to do it. The limited nature of many jobs and the use of ten-man boards reduced the risk of serious failure, though it also provided less scope for those with ability. And the involvement of many citizens in office-holding, including membership of the council (which oversaw the work of the separate offices), meant that those who attended the assembly to make decisions were not an ignorant mob but many of them had experience of public affairs.

Originally justice had been dispensed by individual officials, particularly the nine archons, and by the former archons in the council of the Areopagus; and prosecution had been left to injured parties and their families. Solon had created a category of 'public' lawsuits, in which any citizen could prosecute, and had provided for appeals to a court against the verdicts of individual officials (cf. above). Appeals were perhaps rare at first but became more frequent, and by the 450s (perhaps by gradual development, eventually consolidated by law) appeals had as it were become the norm, so that the archon or other official would simply check that a case was in order and then, rather than give a verdict of his own, take the case automatically to a court in which he presided but did not express an opinion.

There were special procedures for some offences (homicide was still tried by the Areopagus), the travelling justices for minor 'private' cases have been mentioned above, and 'common criminals' who were clearly guilty and admitted it could be put to death without a trial. Charges of major offences against the state could by *eisangelia* ('impeachment') be brought before the council and assembly. In modern states, where the government is strong, it is thought important that the courts should be independent of the government so that they can oblige even the government to obey the laws, but in Athens and other ancient states, where the state was its citizens and the government was weak, it was thought natural that administrative authorities should have judicial powers too, and the council and other authorities were given limited powers of punishment (but had to send the case to a court to obtain more severe punishments).

Litigants had to plead their own cases (they could pay a speech writer, and could enlist supporting speakers, but there were no legal experts), juries were large (always at least 201, and for major cases 1,001 or more), and even the largest cases were decided within a day. Speakers could cite precedents which they thought would help their cases, but there was no systematic recording or invoking of precedents. Jurors had to be thirty years old, like officials, but could come from all four property classes; 6,000 were empanelled each year. The Athenians were notorious for their fondness for litigation (see particularly Aristophanes' comedy *Wasps*), and the extent to which they indulged in it makes it clear that going to a law was a widespread practice, not simply a means by which the élite pursued their feuds.

Whether Athenian courts did indeed apply the law or saw themselves as deciding more generally between opponents has been disputed. I incline in general to the first position, but the availability of such charges as making an illegal proposal (in the council or assembly), and of deceiving the people with false promises, often coupled with an accusation of taking bribes, provided opportunities for attacking politicians and military commanders which did not always distinguish as we might wish between behaviour which was unlawful and behaviour which was unsatisfactory in other ways. And, although public prosecutors could be appointed on occasions (as in the story of Pericles as one of the public prosecutors of Cimon after the war against Thasos: ch. 1), normally prosecution was left to an individual, whether the injured party or *ho boulomenos*, a volunteer citizen, so a wrong might go unpunished if nobody saw fit to prosecute. Athens needed to encourage prosecutors, but not so much as to elicit unjustified prosecutions, and it deployed a mixture of rewards for successful prosecutors and penalties for those who failed to convince even a fifth of the jury. We sometimes encounter references to *sykophantai* (literally '[contraband-]fig-exposers'), men who made a habit of prosecuting in cases in which they were not directly concerned, perhaps in the hope of gaining an official reward or of being paid to settle out of court.

Political life and the role of Pericles

This was an extreme kind of direct democracy, with decisions made by the citizens in the assembly, administration done by large numbers of citizens taking their turn, and amateur law courts with large juries – and citizen involvement on this scale was possible only because there were wives and children, and metics and slaves, who could keep the other wheels of life turning while the adult male citizens devoted themselves to public affairs. Inevitably, not every citizen played his part in accordance with this ideal, but there were some 'quiet Athenians' who avoided public life. However, enough of the citizens were involved in one way or another fairly often to save this system from serious incompetence and chaos, but it was not a system conducive to consistency, in decision- and policy-making, in administration or in the verdicts of the courts.

In the two days of debate on Corcyra and Corinth in 433 the assembly sympathized with Corinth on the first day but decided on limited support for Corcyra on the second (Thuc. I. 44); in 427 (after Pericles' death) the assembly originally decided to kill all the men of Mytilene after suppressing its revolt but on the next day changed to a slightly less severe decision (Thuc. III. 36–49). The decision to include Lacedaemonius, son of Pericles' opponent Cimon, among the generals sent to Corcyra, and the decision to include both Alcibiades, who was enthusiastic for the expedition, and Nicias, who tried to prevent it, among the commanders of the expedition sent to Sicily in 415, probably indicate not that 'the people' wanted a balance among the commanders but that the side which had been defeated in the debate was still strong enough to gain an appointment for one of its men

(Thuc. I. 45. ii, VI. 8; but for different explanations see Plut. *Per.* 29. i–ii, *Nic.* 12. iii–v, *Alc.* 18. i, and Thucydides states that Nicias did not want to be sent to Sicily).

Pericles did not direct Athenian policy, and could not have done so, but between 462/1 and Pericles' death in 429 there was enough agreement within Athens on general objectives, and Pericles was associated with sufficient Athenian policies and actions in different areas, for us to say that the lines which Athens followed – most of the time, though not consistently in every decision and every action – were lines which Pericles encouraged.

But, although Thucydides avoids naming any, Pericles was never without opponents. After Ephialtes' reform of the Areopagus, Cimon was ostracized but Ephialtes was murdered (Plutarch rejected the scandalmonger Idomeneus' claim that Pericles himself killed him out of jealousy: Ideomeneus *FGrH* 338 F 8 *ap.* Plut. *Per.* 10. vii). Even Thucydides reports a rumour of a plot against the democracy at the time of the battle of Tanagra in 458 or 457 (Thuc. I. 107. iv–vi), and Plutarch has a story that Cimon wanted to fight on the Athenian side but was rejected, but afterwards Pericles proposed a decree recalling him from his ostracism (Plut. *Cim.* 17. iv–ix, *Per.* 10. i–iv). However, whatever may be the truth behind those stories, probably Cimon stayed away for the full ten years; for the consequence of his return *c.* 451, see Chapter 3.

Soon afterwards Cimon died in Cyprus, and after that the opposition to Pericles was led by Thucydides, son of Melesias, perhaps a brother-in-law of Cimon and grandfather of Thucydides the historian. According to Plutarch, he focused particularly on Pericles' use of tribute from the Delian League to pay for buildings on the acropolis and elsewhere in Athens (Plut. *Per.* 12–14: cf. chs. 3, 5), and, 'being less of a military man than Cimon, but rather agora-based and political … he did not allow those called the "fine and good" [*kaloi k'agathoi*] to be scattered and mixed with the people, as before … but set them apart and brought them together into the same place'. This resulted in a polarization between the People and the Few (Plut. *Per.* 11). Plutarch seems to mean that he persuaded his supporters to sit together in the assembly, so that they could make their presence felt more effectively, and in principle there is no reason why that should not have happened. There is very little evidence to suggest that Athenians in the assembly habitually voted on class lines, but it is credible that those opposed to the democratic and militarily aggressive policies of Pericles were particularly men of the upper class, even if their objections on particular points, such as Athens' use of the Delian League, were not always class based. According to Plutarch, Pericles offered to pay for the buildings himself – which was far beyond his means – but the assembly gave him its backing. Eventually Thucydides was ostracized: *c.* 444/3, but to insist on that year on the basis of Pericles' fifteen years without a rival in Plut. *Per.* 16. iii is unsafe. And, while Pericles himself was not ostracized, his associate Damon was.

Pericles was subject to further opposition in the 430s, but this time it seems from the democratic end of the spectrum. Pheidias, after completing his statue of Athena for the Parthenon in 438/7, was accused of embezzlement: he fled to Olympia, was commissioned to produce a statue of Zeus there, and ended his life in further trouble. Pericles' consort Aspasia was prosecuted, or perhaps simply attacked in a comedy since the man named as prosecutor was a comedian, for impiety. A religious zealot called Diopithes was the author of a decree making it an offence 'not to believe in divine things or to teach about things up in the air', and it is possible that as a result of that Pericles' friend, the philosopher Anaxagoras, was prosecuted – perhaps in 437/6 and perhaps by the demagogue Cleon – and that he left Athens. Pericles himself was prosecuted, perhaps in connection with the charge against Pheidias: originally an archaic form of trial was proposed, but Hagnon (who had a distinguished public career from the 440s to the 410s) had that changed to an ordinary trial in a court, and presumably Pericles was acquitted (other evidence points to the early 430s for these attacks, but Plut. *Per.* 31. ii–32 mistakenly links them with the outbreak of the Peloponnesian War). Another sign of sensitivity is that between 440/39 and 437/6 a decree 'concerning not comedying' was in force (schol. Ar.

Ach. 67 ~ Fornara 111); but we do not know what it forbade, or why it was first enacted and afterwards annulled.

As we have already noticed, the debate on Corinth and Corcyra in 433 was evenly balanced: it is likely, and Plutarch says so but Thucydides does not, that Pericles was in favour of the eventual decision, to support Corcyra (Thuc. I. 24–55; Plut. *Per.* 29. i–iii). At the beginning of the Peloponnesian War, in 431, some Athenians wanted to go out and give the invaders the battle which Pericles refused to give them (Thuc. II. 21–2). In 430, when the Athenians were suffering from the plague and the invaders came again, the Athenians' morale and willingness to continue fighting were weakened. Envoys were sent to Sparta – which Pericles will have opposed – who tried without success to make peace. Thucydides gives Pericles a speech in defence of his policies; but he was fined and deposed from his generalship, though after a change of mood he was re-elected for the following year (Thuc. II. 59–65. iv; he mentions the fine but not the deposition, which is found in Diod. Sic. XII. 45. iv, Plut. *Per.* 35. iv–v). Pericles was indeed influential for thirty years or more, but in spite of Thucydides' claim there was never a time when he was unquestioned and unrivalled.

We should think, then, of a system in which a large proportion of the citizens played active roles in public life, though not all of them in every year, while a fairly small number were leading politicians who held offices and who made speeches in the law courts year after year. Pericles was one of the latter, and as far as our evidence for particular years goes Plutarch was right to say that from the late 440s to his death he was elected as one of the ten generals every year. He did not 'direct Athenian policy' or control the decisions of the assembly, but he was associated with the various policies which Athens on the whole, though not unwaveringly, pursued.

3

Empire

Precedents

With sufficient land in Attica, Athens was not at first involved in the colonizing activity in which some other Greek states engaged from the eighth century onwards. However, recent work has emphasized that from the beginning of the sixth century it did develop overseas interests. The law attributed to Solon in 594/3 banning the export of natural products other than olive oil (Plut. *Sol.* 24. i–ii) points to an intention to concentrate on what grew well in Attica and to rely on trade rather than self-sufficiency to satisfy its needs, and it was in the sixth century that Athens recovered the lead in fine pottery from Corinth and exported that in increasing quantities.

Throughout the sixth century, Athens challenged Megara for the island of Salamis, in the Saronic Gulf close to the mainland territory of both, and at the end of the century it gained that by arbitration. At the end of the seventh century, Athens fought for, and obtained by arbitration, Sigeum, just outside the mouth of the Hellespont; and, after subsequently losing it, it reconquered that in the middle of the century. Probably also Athens gained possession of Elaeus, just inside the Hellespont on the Chersonese. In the middle of the century, Miltiades (step-uncle of the Miltiades who was to fight at Marathon) accepted an invitation to reinforce a settlement of Thracian Dolonci in the Chersonese. According to Herodotus, he went because he did not want to live in Athens under Pisistratus' rule (Hdt. VI. 34–7), but he must have gone with some degree of approval from Pisistratus; members of his family continued to rule there until the 490s. In the Aegean,

Lygdamis of Naxos helped Pisistratus to seize power in Athens, and Pisistratus in turn helped him to become tyrant of Naxos. Pisistratus took an interest in the Ionians' sacred island of Delos, 'purifying' it by removing bodies buried within sight of the sanctuary.

In the last quarter of the sixth century, Greek states began adopting as their warships triremes, ships with three banks of oars and a total crew of about 200 (cf. fig. 3.1). Only exceptionally rich men could afford a trireme of their own, so (while the earlier, smaller ships may largely have been owned by rich individuals) these ships were state funded and state owned, and it is likely that the navy of fifty ships with which Athens began the fifth century was a navy of triremes.

At the end of the sixth century, Athens began to tangle with the Persians, who had conquered western Asia Minor in the middle of the century and had become the leading power in the near east. After falling out with Sparta over its opposition to Cleisthenes, Athens sought an alliance with Persia, but it had second thoughts when Persia demanded earth and water as formal tokens of submission; and when the expelled tyrant Hippias took refuge with the Persians Athens protested. Athens

Figure 3.1 *Olympias*, replica trireme.

was regarded as the mother city of the Ionians, the Greeks who had settled in the central part of the Aegean and of the coast of Asia Minor; and it was no doubt partly on account of that, partly on account of Athens' recent experiences of the Persians, and partly a sign of ambition, that in 499 Athens accepted an invitation to support the Ionian Revolt against Persia. Twenty Athenian ships (and five from Eretria, in the island of Euboea) were sent in 498; the Athenians withdrew after that year (and we cannot be sure why); but when in 494 the revolt was put down and Miletus was sacked, Phrynichus wrote a tragedy about that, and the Athenians were distressed because it 'reminded them of evils which were their own' (Hdt. VI. 21. ii).

The Persians began to take an interest in the lands to the north of the Aegean before 510. How soon they began to think of mainland Greece is not clear, but they were starting to take in distinguished refugees from Greece (an exiled Spartan king as well as Hippias). It is possible that the heralds sent to demand the formal submission of the Greeks were sent in 493/2, rather than 492/1, the context in which Herodotus mentions them (Hdt. VI. 48–49. i). At any rate, the support of Eretria and Athens for the Ionian Revolt provided an excuse for an attack on Greece, if the Persians thought they needed one, and they were the targets of the Persian invasion of Greece in 490.

After Eretria was betrayed to them, the Persians (accompanied by Hippias) crossed from Euboea to Attica and landed near Marathon. The Athenians sent out their full army to face the Persians; they received help from neighbouring Plataea, and the Spartans promised help but did not send it immediately. A battle was fought in which the Athenians were victorious. When the Persians sailed round to the coast near Athens, they found that the Athenian army had arrived before them, and so they withdrew. This success won almost on their own was a great source of pride for the Athenians.

Since before 500 Athens had been engaged in intermittent warfare against the island state of Aegina, in the middle of the Saronic Gulf. In 483/2 Themistocles persuaded the Athenians to spend profits from their silver mines on new triremes, rather than pay a dividend to the citizens (there were precedents from other Greek states for both). Ostensibly, these ships were built for the war against Aegina. They gave Athens a navy of 200 ships, more than half of the Greek total, to contribute to the resistance when the Persians invaded Greece again, in 480; but it is perhaps more likely that this was good luck for Themistocles' reputation than that as early as that he could foresee a Persian War in which navies would play a large part.

The Persians did want to avenge their defeat at Marathon, but Greece was not their only concern and they took their time. They assembled large forces for a parallel invasion by land and sea, and King Xerxes himself commanded, travelling to Sardis in western Asia Minor in 481. The first signs of Greek preparation are in the autumn of that year, with an attempt to build up an anti-Persian alliance (which by no means all Greek states joined) and Sparta accepted as the leader. In 480 a first Greek attempt to oppose the Persians in Thessaly had to be abandoned. A small army trying to block the Persians' land route in the narrows of Thermopylae was defeated when the Persians found a way round the Greeks' position, while the Greek navy fought a holding action off Artemisium, at the north end of Euboea, but had to withdraw when Thermopylae fell.

That left all Greece, as far as the Isthmus of Corinth, open to the invaders: the Athenians abandoned Attica, which was overrun by the Persians. The Greek navy was now based on Salamis. Some southern Greeks wanted to withdraw to the Peloponnese, but the Persians would then have been able to attack them city by city. Before that withdrawal could happen, Themistocles allegedly sent a deceitful message to Xerxes, and so managed to bring about a battle in the straits between mainland Attica and Salamis, in which the Greeks were victorious. This happened probably about the end of September. Part of the Persian army was left in Greece, but Xerxes with the rest, and the Persian navy, withdrew. In 479 the Athenians eventually persuaded the Spartans and other Peloponnesians to venture north of the isthmus, and the remaining Persian army was defeated at Plataea. The Greek navy (with Pericles' father Xanthippus commanding the Athenian contingent), encouraged by eastern Greeks, crossed the Aegean, landed on Cape Mycale, facing the island of Samos, and defeated the Persians there. After that the Greeks went north to the Hellespont, where they found Xerxes' bridges already broken by storms. The Peloponnesians then returned home, but the Athenians and others, under Xanthippus, stayed on and captured Sestos, on the European side of the Hellespont.

The growth of the Delian League

The Greeks will have assumed that, just as the Persians had returned after their defeat at Marathon, they would return again after their defeat in 480–479. In 478 fighting against the Persians continued around the Aegean, again under Spartan leadership, but the misconduct of the Spartan commander Pausanias prompted the taking of the lead by Athens and the withdrawal of Sparta. Athens had been taking an interest in the eastern Greeks. After the battle of Mycale, it had successfully opposed a Peloponnesian proposal that they should be transplanted to new homes on land to be confiscated from states in Greece which had supported the Persians (Hdt. IX. 106. ii–iv), and it had the naval capacity for an overseas war. Our sources disagree over whether the initiative came from Athens or from the other Greeks, but there must have been willingness on both sides, and it could not have been predicted that Pausanias would provide the opportunity for this change.

Thucydides gives a short account of the organization of the Delian League (its modern name: the headquarters was originally on the sacred island of Delos). 'The pretext was to obtain recompense for what they had suffered by ravaging the King's land' (though surely the objectives also included liberating Greek states still under Persian rule and preventing further hostile action by Persia). Allies either contributed their own ships to the League's forces or paid annual 'tribute' in cash. 'The Athenians were the leaders of allies who at first were autonomous [probably that was assumed rather than spelled out, since it did not occur to anybody that the allies might not be autonomous] and deliberated in common meetings' (Thuc. I. 96. i–97. i). Other texts indicate that at any rate the assessment of the allies' obligations was the work of the Athenian Aristides, and that the alliance was intended as a full and permanent offensive and defensive alliance, 'to have the same friends and enemies'. This was comparable to Sparta's alliance, the Peloponnesian League, but within a Greek alliance the collection of tribute was new (though Persia and other near-eastern states had collected tribute from their subjects). Another novelty emerged as it became clear that Athens took this permanent alliance to involve permanent warfare, year after year. For a small state the burden of contributing to annual campaigns was heavy: in the end almost all the members agreed to pay tribute rather than provide their own forces, and that development put more power in the Athenians' hands.

In part of his Book I, Thucydides gives a short account of events in the *pentekontaetia*, the (almost) fifty years between the Persian Wars and the Peloponnesian War. It is a selective account, and is designed to substantiate Thucydides' view that the most important reason for the Peloponnesian War was that 'the Athenians by becoming great and inspiring fear in the Spartans forced them to go to war' (Thuc. I. 89. i–118. ii; reason for war 23. v–vi, 88, 118. ii). Other texts mostly give more information on the same events rather than add further events.

Not surprisingly, the events which we know of do show how the Athenians used the Delian League to build up their power. Early campaigns were against the Persians or Greeks who had supported them, but from the beginning the Athenians found ways of advancing their own interests as well. The first recorded campaign, to capture Eïon on the Thracian coast from the Persians, was followed by the settlement of Eïon as an Athenian colony (Plut. *Cim.* 7. iii: colony not mentioned by Thuc. I. 98. i). The second was against Scyros, in the northern Aegean: that is not known to have been involved in the Persian Wars, but it was in a crucial position on the route between the Hellespont and Athens, and the Athenians brought back from it what they claimed to be the skeleton of the legendary hero Theseus, and settled Scyros as a colony too (Thuc. I. 98. ii; Theseus Plut. *Cim.* 8. iii–vii). Most spectacular of the early successes against the Persians was the victory by land and sea, perhaps in 469, at the mouth of the River Eurymedon, on the south coast of Asia Minor not far west of Cyprus (Thuc. I. 100. i). We can assume that, as the Delian League came to dominate the Aegean, more and more states judged it better to join the League than to oppose it. But disquiet soon arose, probably already in the 470s, the large island state of Naxos tried to defect but was forced back into the League. Thucydides writes that 'this was the first allied city to be enslaved contrary to what had been established, but afterwards it happened individually to the others too'; and he comments that the main reason for defection was reluctance to provide ships or tribute year after year, 'for the Athenians enforced the obligations punctiliously' (Thuc. I. 98. iv–99). 'Enslaved' is to be understood metaphorically (probably Naxos was treated much as Thasos was to be treated later: cf. below), but the Athenians increasingly behaved as superiors rather than as leaders of equal allies. From 465/4 to 463/2 Athens confronted another defection, of Thasos, off the Thracian coast, 'owing to a dispute about the trading posts in Thrace opposite and about the mine which they administered', which Athens presumably was claiming for itself. Eventually Thasos capitulated, demolishing its city wall, surrendering its navy, paying tribute in cash and giving up the mainland sites and the mine (Thuc. I. 100. ii–101).

In these campaigns, the League's commander wherever known was Cimon, who in contrast to Themistocles envisaged a world in which Athens and Sparta could co-exist. Thucydides reports that when Thasos revolted it appealed for support to Sparta, and Sparta secretly promised to help but was unable to do so because of the earthquake of *c.* 464/3 and the helot revolt for which that provided an opportunity (Thuc. I. 101. i–ii). An alleged promise which was secret and was not kept arouses suspicion, and it may be that this was invented later to help explain why Sparta did not stop the growth of Athens while that was still feasible. For help against the helots Sparta asked its allies, including Athens. As we have seen (cf. ch. 1), Cimon had himself sent with soldiers, but in his absence Ephialtes had his democratic reform passed by the assembly, and the Spartans, worried by Athens' change of direction, dismissed Cimon and the Athenians. Cimon was ostracized, and the Athenians broke off their alliance with Sparta, made alliances with enemies of Sparta, and while not abandoning their war against Persia added to it an attempt to gain power in mainland Greece (Thuc. I. 102).

From this point onwards we have evidence for the Delian League not only in Thucydides' history and other literary texts but also in inscriptions, particularly decrees and other documents of the Athenian state. Often what survives is incomplete and has to be reconstructed, and for many decrees we do not have an unambiguous statement of the date. Over the course of the fifth century, the form in which the Athenians carved certain letters of their alphabet changed. For a long time it was believed that any text with the older forms of lettering should be dated not later than *c.* 445, and on that basis a number of texts reflecting what was seen as a harsh form of imperialism were dated about the middle of the century. A lengthy campaign against that belief suggested that many of the harsh documents should in fact be dated up to thirty years later. It does now seem clear that some cutters continued to use older forms of letters until after 420; but this means not that later dates must be preferred for all such inscriptions but only that later dates must not be ruled out *a priori*. I believe that the later dates suggested are right for some of the inscriptions but not for all of them; and, while it is arguable that in some respects Athenian imperialism went further in the 420s, it had already reached an advanced stage by the middle of the century.

Thucydides proceeds to interweave two narratives covering *c.* 460–454: a campaign to support an Egyptian ruler rebelling against the Persians (there had been Greeks settling in and trading with Egypt since the seventh century), which ended in failure and the loss of large forces; and (after Megara, on the isthmus between Athens and Corinth and currently at odds with Corinth, had aligned itself with Athens) fighting against Aegina and on the Greek mainland, in what is called the First Peloponnesian War. That war led to the addition of Aegina to the League and to territorial gains for Athens in Boeotia and neighbouring regions of central Greece. In the course of it the Athenians built the long walls which linked the harbour town of Piraeus to Athens in a single fortified area; and Thucydides mentions for the first time, *c.* 454, an expedition commanded by Pericles, into the Gulf of Corinth from Megara (Thuc. I. 103. iv–111).

But after *c.* 454 Athens failed to make further gains in Greece, and the Persians may have been encouraged by their success in Egypt to attempt a recovery in Asia Minor: an Athenian decree imposing a democratic constitution on Erythrae, probably in the late 450s, seems to indicate that Athens had regained control there after a Persian-backed revolt (*IG* i³ 14 = O&R 121 ~ Fornara 71: cf. ch. 2). Apparently in 454/3, the Athenians moved the treasury of the League from Delos to Athens. According to Plut. *Arist.* 25. iii, this was done on the proposal of Samos, and it may have been prompted by anxiety about Persia and the Aegean. Offerings were now made to Athena of ¹/₆₀ of the tribute (perhaps previously an offering had been made to Delian Apollo), and beginning in 454/3 the Athenians inscribed lists of these offerings, calculated separately on each member state's tribute, on a block of stone so large that it eventually held fourteen lists (*IG* i³ 259–72; extracts O&R 119 ~ Fornara 85). Cimon returned to Athens probably in 451, ten years after he was ostracized, and probably his presence in Athens facilitated a five-year treaty with the Peloponnesians which was made in 451/0. He then led a campaign to Cyprus, which had a mixed Greek and non-Greek population, and in which both the Greeks and the Persians took an interest, but he was killed there (Thuc. I. 112. i–iv).

The Delian League as an Athenian empire

After Cimon's death, regular warfare against Persia ceased. From the fourth century onwards we encounter frequent references to a Peace of Callias, by which the Persians abandoned all claims to the Aegean and western Asia Minor, but Thucydides says nothing at this point and there is no unambiguous fifth-century evidence for such a treaty. I am one of the minority who find it hard to believe that the Persians would have agreed to such a treaty, and I think that it was invented after the King's Peace of 387/6, which returned the Greek cities of Asia Minor to Persia and established Persia as the underwriter of a settlement among the Greeks, in order to make more real the contrast between the glory of Athens' past achievements and the disgrace of its acquiescence in the King's Peace.

Although no longer fighting against Persia, Athens kept the League in being. Plutarch reports a proposal of Pericles to create a new league of all the Greeks, which came to nothing when Sparta refused the invitation, and I think that there would have been no point in inventing an invitation which achieved nothing, and that this invitation is to be believed (Plut. *Per.* 17). The tribute lists of the years around 450 show marked differences between one year and the next, which may reflect the reluctance of some members to pay. And there was one year for which there is no list: between what was certainly list 5 (450/49) and what was certainly list 10 (445/4) there are not four lists but only three; probably the missing list is what should be list 6 (449/8), but afterwards the Athenians continued to number the lists as if there had been one for that year. Often this has been linked with the uncertainties about the future of the League, but an explanation of another kind is possible. The orator Antiphon mentions an occasion when all the *hellenotamiai* ('Greek treasurers', the Athenians' treasurers of the League) were judged guilty of embezzlement and sentenced to death; but after all but one had been executed the true explanation (we do not know what that was) was discovered (Antiph. V. *Herodes* 69–71). It has been suggested that that occurred in 449/8 and that the absence of list 6 is due to the problems of that year rather than to uncertainty about the future of the League.

After the treasury was moved from Delos to Athens, regular meetings of the allies seem to have been discontinued: we hear no more of them, and Athens on its own appears to have taken decisions which we should expect to be taken by the whole alliance if meetings were still held. When member states caused trouble, Athens reacted firmly, sometimes installing 'cleruchs' (allotment-holders) who remained

Athenian citizens but were given land in an allied state's territory, sometimes interfering in a state's internal arrangements, as in the imposition of a democratic constitution on Erythrae. However, while democratic Athens preferred democracy in allied states, it did not systematically impose democratic constitutions throughout the League, but intervened only where provocation and opportunity offered. In due course all member states, not only those which were Ionian in the strict sense and could be regarded as settled from Athens, were required to send offerings to major religious festivals in Athens, and some categories of lawsuit were transferred from local courts to Athenian courts, which could be expected to favour pro-Athenian litigants.

In the early 440s, Athens started erecting new buildings on the acropolis and elsewhere, after leaving in ruins for thirty years the temples which the Persians had destroyed in 480–479: the first year of the annual accounts of the overseers of the Parthenon, inscribed on another large block of stone, was 447/6 (*IG* i³ 436–51; extracts O&R 145 ~ Fornara 120: cf. ch. 5). It is possible that in some way surplus tribute was reassigned to the building programme; in any case, since Athens was no longer fighting every year, it had more money for other purposes. As we have seen, this was the issue on which Thucydides, son of Melesias, based his opposition to Pericles. According to Plutarch, he claimed that tribute which had been collected for fighting against the Persians was being spent on gilding and tarting up Athens like a wanton woman; and Pericles replied that, as long as Athens kept the allies safe from the Persians, it did not have to account to them for the money (Plut. *Per.* 12–14: cf. ch. 2).

Athens' five-year truce with the Peloponnesians held more or less (a 'sacred war' over Delphi did not break it, since Sparta and Athens conducted separate campaigns and did not fight against each other). However, in 447/6 rebellions began close to Athens. Boeotia revolted after about ten years of Athenian control, and defeated an Athenian army and succeeded in asserting its independence. Then the cities of Euboea revolted: Pericles led a force to Euboea, and while he was there Megara defected and Sparta led a Peloponnesian invasion of

Attica. Pericles returned to Athens. The Peloponnesians withdrew from Attica, and it was believed both in Sparta (which exiled its king Pleistoanax) and in Athens (where Pericles was said to have included in his accounts a sum of ten talents 'for what was necessary') that Pericles had bribed them to do so. What he perhaps had done was not bribe the Spartans to withdraw but undertake that Athens would agree to the terms which it subsequently did agree to. Pericles went back to Euboea and restored Athenian control there, but in 446/5 Athens made the Thirty Years' Peace with Sparta, by which it gave up the territories which it had gained on the Greek mainland (Thuc. I. 112. v–115. i).

That seemed to represent a victory for Sparta, but it did in effect recognize the division of the Greek world into two power blocs, a Spartan based on the Greek mainland and an Athenian based on the Aegean. What had by now become an Athenian empire was substantially intact. And it soon became apparent that Athens was still eager to expand wherever it could do so outside Sparta's area of influence. Signs of continuing Athenian ambition included the foundation of Thurii in place of the former Sybaris, in southern Italy, *c.* 444/3, and further north in Italy involvement in a refoundation of Neapolis; alliances with Rhegium on the toe of Italy and Leontini in Sicily; the foundation of a colony at Amphipolis, in Thrace inland from Eïon, in 437/6 (but Athens had been interested in the site since the 470s); and support for a refoundation of Amphilochian Argos, in north-western Greece, perhaps in the early 430s. Perhaps in the mid-430s, Pericles himself led an expedition to the Black Sea and founded a colony at Sinope on its south coast; and Athens made an alliance with the Spartocid kings of the Cimmerian Bosporus (Crimea), an important source of grain.

There is only one episode after 446/5 which Thucydides mentions in his account of the *pentekontaetia*. In 440–439 Athens supported Miletus when it was at war against Samos (it was alleged that Pericles had been influenced in that decision by the Milesian Aspasia). Samos was one of the few Delian League members which did not pay tribute but still contributed its own ships; it had support from Persia (so if there was a Peace of Callias the Persians were breaking it); and the Corinthians when trying to dissuade Athens from its alliance with Corcyra (cf. below) are represented by Thucydides as claiming that they had prevented the Peloponnesian League from giving support to Samos (which must mean that Sparta had been willing to give such support). Pericles was one of the Athenian commanders; Samos posed a serious threat, and Athens had to use large forces, but Samos was eventually defeated and lost its privileged ship-providing status (Thuc. I. 114. ii–117. iii; Peloponnesian League 40. v).

The Peloponnesian War

Thucydides begins his account of the events leading to the Peloponnesian War with a dispute between Corinth and its colony Corcyra, off the coast of north-western Greece. In 433, Corcyra asked Athens for an alliance, Corinth argued against granting it, Athens then made a purely defensive alliance with Corcyra (so that it would not be dragged into an undeniable breach of the Thirty Years' Peace), and Athenian forces were sent and in the event had to intervene to save Corcyra from defeat. Athens' decision was close: Thucydides does not name Pericles or any other Athenian, but Plutarch thought, surely correctly, that Pericles did favour supporting Corcyra (Thuc. I. 24–55, Plut. *Per.* 29. i–iii). About the same time, Athens wound up the acropolis building programme and put its sacred funds (on which it would draw to finance the war) in order: outstanding debts to the sacred treasuries were repaid, and the funds of many gods other than Athena were amalgamated in a single treasury of the Other Gods, to be kept on the acropolis with the treasury of Athena (*IG* i³ 52 = O&R 144 ~ Fornara 119: best dated 434/3, though other dates have been proposed). Also, expecting a war in which the west would be involved, Athens reaffirmed its alliances with Rhegium and Leontini (*IG* i³ 53–4 = O&R 149 ~ Fornara 124–5).

Next Athens put pressure on Potidaea, in the north-west of the Aegean, a colony of Corinth but a member of the Delian League. That again led to fighting between Athens and Corinth – or rather Corinthian volunteers: here it looks as if Corinth was trying to avoid an undeniable breach of the Peace (Thuc. I. 56–66). Corinth led member states of the Peloponnesian League in trying to arouse Sparta; further grievances against Athens arose from Megara, which Athens was subjecting to economic sanctions on account of a boundary dispute, and Aegina, which complained that Athens was not allowing it the autonomy which it had promised. Thucydides gives us a speech by Athenians in Sparta which is unapologetic about Athenian power and warns the Spartans not to go to war against Athens lightly. Archidamus, one of Sparta's kings, wanted to play for time, but Sthenelaïdas, one of the ephors, gained support for a proposal that they should go to war unless Athens backed down; and Thucydides thought that Sparta was persuaded by its fear of Athenian power rather than by the particular complaints (Thuc. I. 67–88).

That decision was confirmed by a formal vote of the Peloponnesian League. The winter of 432/1 was devoted to exchanges of propaganda. The Spartans tried to invoke the curse on the Alcmaeonid family, from the seventh century (cf. ch. 2), against Pericles, and the Athenians responded with Spartan curses. They then urged Athens to give way on the particular complaints, especially that of Megara, and finally and more fundamentally to allow the Greeks their freedom (Thuc. I. 119–39). Thucydides had already said of Pericles that 'in leading the state he was totally opposed to the Spartans, and would not allow the Athenians to give way but impelled them towards the war' (Thuc. I. 127. iii), and he ended Book I with the first of the speeches which he put in Pericles' mouth: appeasement would not work; if war had to come, let it come, and Athens was ready for it (Thuc. I. 140–5) – or, as G. W. Hunt put it, in a music hall song of the 1870s in connection with a British warning to Russia:

We don't want to fight, but by jingo! if we do,
We've got the ships, we've got the men, we've got the money too.

Thucydides gave his account of the war 'so that no one should ever need to ask from what origin so great a war broke out among the Greeks' (Thuc. I. 23. v), but the question has been debated ever since. My own view is that Athens' actions after 446/5 showed it still to be too ambitious for Sparta's comfort, and that as the war approached the Athenians, and Pericles in particular, were not willing to back down, but thought that if war had to come it should come when they could claim to be technically in the right and when they were better prepared than their opponents.

The war began in 431. First the Thebans made a pre-emptive but unsuccessful strike on Athens' Boeotian ally Plataea, which gave Athens a grievance against the Spartan bloc (Thuc. II. 2–6). Then, after sending a herald whom the Athenians rejected, Sparta's king Archidamus with a Peloponnesian army formally invaded Attica. If the war had proceeded in the typical Greek manner, the Athenians would have gone out of the city to fight the invaders, and, with inferior land forces, would have been beaten. But Athens was as much superior at sea as the Peloponnesians on land, and the long walls joining Athens to Piraeus made of them a single fortified area. Pericles therefore urged on the Athenians an unusual strategy: they should abandon the countryside and allow that to be overrun, while they stayed inside the fortifications and relied on their sea power to import what they needed from abroad and to make counter-raids on the Peloponnese. This would not bring quick victory, but the Athenians with their ample financial resources could outlast the Peloponnesians, and Thucydides attributes to Pericles a remarkable speech in which he gives the Athenians a review of their resources. Pericles himself had connections with Archidamus, and, fearing that the invaders might deliberately spare his property, he offered to give that up to the state if this happened: we do not know if his property was spared and was given to the state (Thuc. II. 7–17).

Pericles' strategy has in fact given rise to problems. The counter-raids on the Peloponnese in 431 and 430, although Thucydides reports them in a perfunctory way, were on a very large scale, which to most scholars has seemed inconsistent with Thucydides' defensive emphasis. And we have an inscription which records the Athenians' borrowings from the sacred treasuries between 433 and 422, which allows us to calculate that in the first two or three years of the war they were using up their money at a rate which would not have allowed them to keep going for long: only after Pericles' death did they attempt to increase their income and reduce their expenditure (*IG* i³ 369 = O&R 160 ~ extracts Fornara 134). Different explanations have been suggested, and my own is that Pericles was cautious in his public pronouncements and that Thucydides reflects them, but privately he hoped, mistakenly, that after a few years of making no headway against Athens the Peloponnesians would admit that they could not win. Not in any of the speeches but in his final comment on Pericles Thucydides attributes to him the advice that they should 'not try to add to their empire during the war or put the city at risk' (Thuc. II. 65. vii). The Athenians certainly departed from that advice after Pericles' death, most strikingly in Sicily in 427–424 and 415–413, but there were smaller exceptions even while Pericles was alive (in 431, Thuc. II. 26. ii, 30; in 430, II. 56).

In 431 some Athenians wanted to go out and give the invaders the battle which Pericles refused to give them (Thuc. II. 21–2). In 430, when Athens was hit by the plague and the Peloponnesians invaded again, the Athenians were less enthusiastic for the war, and – surely in the face of opposition from Pericles – they sent envoys to Sparta who tried without success to make peace. Thucydides gives Pericles another speech, in defence of his policies; but he was fined and deposed from his generalship, though after a change of mood he was re-elected for 430/29 (Thuc. II. 59–65. iv: cf. ch. 2), and, we should assume, was elected again for 429/8. He makes no further appearance in Thucydides' narrative, and he died in the autumn of 429. There is no further sign that any Athenians were interested in making peace until the truce of 423 (cf. ch. 6).

When Pericles died, Athens was firmly in control of an empire the like of which had not existed among the Greeks before. It saw itself, with some justification, as the strongest power in Greece; its strength and ambition had alarmed the Spartans, and it had decided to risk war against them rather than give way in the face of their complaints. The war had begun as a war of non-encounter, which confirmed the superiority of the Athenians at sea and of the Spartans on land; but it seemed that the Athenians, if they did not challenge the Spartans where the Spartans were strong, could not be defeated.

4

Religion and Philosophy

Religion

According to Herodotus, the Athenians said in 479 to the Spartans, to explain why they could not desert the Greek cause and support the Persians, that *to Hellenikon*, the Greek people, was of the same blood and spoke the same language, and they had common sanctuaries of the gods and sacrifices, and similar customs (Hdt. VIII. 144. ii). The Greeks had many gods and goddesses (with no finite list: new deities could be introduced), and had stories in which they behaved and misbehaved very much like human beings but on a larger scale. They were believed to interact with the mortal world in various ways, sometimes to reward the good and to punish the wicked, but sometimes in a more partisan way to support their friends and harm their enemies. As I remarked in Chapter 1, there was general agreement among the Greeks in different places on the principal gods, and there were some sanctuaries with their festivals which had more than a local appeal (particularly that of Zeus at Olympia and that of Apollo at Delphi; in Attica, that of Demeter and Persephone at Eleusis). Although these attracted dedications and worshippers from non-Greeks, they saw themselves as catering primarily for Greeks: Herodotus reports that early in the fifth century Alexander I of Macedon entered for the foot race at Olympia, the other Greeks wanted to exclude him as being not Greek but barbarian, but he convinced the officials that he was a Greek, of Argive descent (Hdt. V. 22: whether that claim was justified need not concern us here).

But, in religious matters as in other matters, underneath an overall similarity there was an endless variety of local differences. In each city particular gods were particularly favoured, and there were distinctive local features of their cult. Athena in Athens was not exactly the same as Athena in Sparta, and indeed within Athens and Attica there were various sanctuaries of Athena, where she was worshipped under different cult titles with different rituals on different occasions.

To limit ourselves to the acropolis in Athens, by the end of the fifth century there were on it statues which were independent of any temple: these statues were of Athena Promachos ('who fights in front'), said to have been financed from the spoils taken from the Persians at Marathon, and the 'Lemnian Athena', marking the sending of further Athenian settlers to the north-Aegean island of Lemnos *c.* 450. There was an 'ancient' temple of Athena, between the later Parthenon and Erechtheum, built early in the sixth century, rebuilt in the middle of the century and damaged by the Persians in 480–479. The Parthenon, built between 447/6 and 433/2 on the site of an earlier temple which was under construction at the time of the Persian invasion, was the temple of Athena Parthenos ('maiden'), who was also Athena Polias ('of the city'): it housed Pheidias' gold and ivory statue of Athena, but it was not a conventional temple in front of which religious rites were celebrated. The temple of Athena Nike ('victory') was built on a bastion at the south-west corner of the acropolis, perhaps planned in the 440s at the beginning of the work on the acropolis but actually built some time after. The Erechtheum, a complex building on the northern part of the acropolis, which housed a number of cults and objects, including the ancient cult statue of Athena, was begun perhaps *c.* 420 and completed in 405/4. (On statues and buildings cf. ch. 5.)

Willingness to worship a god presupposes some beliefs about that god and about the efficacy of the worship offered, but in Greek religion there were no sacred texts which had a privileged status, and variations between standard stories as presented in different works of literature show that there was no approved body of doctrine to which one had to subscribe. One demonstrated one's devotion to the gods by taking part in the right actions on the right occasions, in the city or in a sanctuary with wider appeal, and in smaller groups of various kinds within the city, and in the family, in order to maintain a good relationship between the god and the human worshippers. We have inscribed calendars of religious observances not only for Athens and other cities but also for demes and other kinds of smaller group. What we think of as typical Greek acts of worship (though they were by no means peculiar to the Greeks) are processions and, often as the climax of a procession, sacrifices – of animals which might be burnt whole (the original meaning of the word 'holocaust') so that everything went to the god, or from which meat might be available for worshippers to feast on and skins might be available for leather; various kinds of vegetable offering and libations of wine might be made too. Prayers were made in various contexts, for instance at the beginning of meetings of the assembly. Offerings were made at sanctuaries in fulfilment of vows or in thanksgiving for benefits which the god was believed to have conferred.

There were also rituals which to us in our context seem stranger: for instance, the weaving of a new robe which every four years was taken in the Panathenaic procession as the sail of a ship-like vehicle, and then used to clothe the old cult statue of Athena; and the drinking competition at the *Choes* ('beakers'), the second day of the festival of new wine known as Anthesteria. And religious festivals could include other elements which in our societies are not associated with religion, such as competitions in the musical performance of drama and other literary compositions, and in various kinds of athletic activity.

'Mystery' cults, such as that of Demeter and Kore ('the girl': Persephone) at Eleusis, involved initiation and/or participation in intense experiences which gave a feeling of communion with the deity. Athens had not in the sixth century managed to achieve panhellenic status for its patriotic festival of Athena, the Panathenaea, to match the festivals at Olympia, Delphi, Nemea and the Isthmus of Corinth (though in the later decades of the Delian League it required member states to send offerings to the Great Panathenaea: cf. below), but the Eleusinian mysteries did succeed in gaining that broader appeal to the Greek world as a whole.

The gods gave advice and indications of their wishes through oracles and through omens of various kinds (meteorological phenomena, the state of the liver of a sacrificial animal, and so on), but they did not give direct orders to communities or to individuals. A sudden happening such as an eclipse might be thought to portend something, but human beings would have to assess what that might be. Otherwise, it was normal to seek the will and the favour of the gods on various occasions (such as founding a colony, or embarking on a war), but it was for the communities and individuals to decide when and in what way to do that. If an oracle was asked whether it was better to do *A* or *B*, the answer was straightforward, but many responses and signs required interpretation, and the oracle at Delphi gained a reputation for giving ambiguous responses. Before the Persian invasion in 480, according to Herodotus, when the Athenians consulted Delphi, the first advice was to flee; when they asked for a more favourable oracle, they were given a response which again advised flight but which also mentioned a wooden wall and 'divine Salamis'. This was discussed by the assembly, and some men thought that the wooden wall referred to a fence round the acropolis, but Themistocles persuaded the Athenians to interpret the wooden wall as the navy's ships, and to regard 'divine' rather than 'cruel Salamis' as an indication that Salamis would play a good role for the Athenians (Hdt. VII. 140–3).

Religion was 'embedded' in Greek society, as Christianity used to be embedded in European societies and societies of European colonists elsewhere but is not today, whereas religion is still embedded in some of the world's other societies today. The Greeks could distinguish between sacred and secular (for instance, in Athens the treasury of Athena and the other sacred treasuries were distinct from the secular funds of the state and of the Delian League, and religious matters formed a separate category of business in the assembly's agenda), but religion was bound up with the lives of communities and individuals in such a way that it was not a separate area, for people who chose to be religious, but was an integral part of every aspect of everybody's life. Assemblies and other decision-making bodies decided religious questions as they decided other questions. Priests and other religious functionaries were officials of the community just like secular officials, except insofar as there might be distinctive rules about eligibility and tenure for religious appointments (we shall see below that democratic Athens departed from previous rules in these respects for newly created religious positions).

Thucydides represents Pericles as claiming in his funeral oration that Athens has provided 'the greatest number of relaxations from toil for the spirit, by holding contests and sacrifices throughout the year' (Thuc. II. 38. i); and the 'Old Oligarch' states that the Athenians hold 'more festivals than any of the Greek states', or, no doubt with exaggeration, 'twice as many festivals as the others do' ([Xen.] *Ath. Pol.* iii. 2, 8). Probably the Athenians were not an exceptionally religious people, but the size of the city and its openness to influences from various places had led to an exceptional accumulation of observances towards various deities for the whole city and for groups within it. (At least as regards religious impediments to action, it seems to have been the Spartans who were exceptionally observant.) The city of Athens had nearly 150 festival days in the year (though many of them were days when the assembly did not meet but the council and the law courts still did), and to them we must add festivals of subsidiary units within the city.

There are two particular features of Athenian religion in the time of Pericles which deserve notice. First, when a new priestess of Athena Nike was instituted, perhaps in the 440s, the assembly decreed that the appointment should be made 'from all Athenian women' (*IG* i³ 35 = O&R 137 ~ Fornara 93. 3–5). All Athenian priesthoods instituted earlier than this had been appointed from the members of a particular *genos* (an extended family, albeit with a fictitious rather than an actual remotest ancestor), but this and all known priesthoods instituted subsequently were open to all Athenian men or women. It has indeed been suggested that one purpose of Pericles' requiring all citizens to be fully Athenian in that they had both an Athenian father and an Athenian mother was that they should be properly eligible for appointment to priesthoods. That priestess, like priests instituted earlier, may have served for life, but at least some of the priests instituted later served for a single year, like most secular officials. This is the one respect in which the religion of democratic Athens acquired a distinctively democratic character.

Secondly, we must notice the religious dimensions of the Delian League. Athens sometimes represented the members of the League as Ionians (strictly, the strand of the Greek people who had settled in the central Aegean and on the central part of Asia Minor's Aegean coast), though not all of the members, even at first, were Ionians in that strict sense. Athens was regarded as the mother city of the Ionians, from which they had set out for their current homes during the dark age *c.* 1000, and so it could claim to be the proper leader of an Ionian league as Sparta was the proper leader of its predominantly Dorian Peloponnesian League. The original headquarters of the League was Apollo's sacred island of Delos, which attracted worshippers particularly from the Ionians and the other eastern Greeks. Probably an offering from the tribute was at first given to Delian Apollo, as it was later given to Athena in Athens. In the earlier decades of the League's history, a new temple of Apollo (the 'peripteral temple') was under construction on Delos; but that was discontinued about the time when the League's treasury was moved to Athens, and was not resumed until the late fourth century, though the 'Athenian temple' was built between that and the 'archaic temple' of the sixth century in the years after 425.

After the treasury had been moved, the tribute was brought to Athens year by year before the Great Dionysia in the spring, and displayed at that festival. From about the middle of the century we have evidence in inscriptions that Athens was requiring member states to send offerings to festivals in Athens: at first, perhaps, only those states which were Ionian in the strict sense and could be regarded as colonies of Athens (e.g. Erythrae to send grain [?] to the Great Panathenaea, late 450s: *IG* i³ 14 = O&R 121 ~ Fornara 71. 2–5), but later all the member states (e.g. first fruits of grain to Eleusis demanded from League members and invited from other Greeks, 430s: *IG* i³ 78 = O&R 141 ~ Fornara 140; a cow and a suit of armour to be sent to the Great Panathenaea by all members, 425/4: *IG* i³71 = O&R 153 ~ Fornara 136. 55–8).

In some of the member states, *horoi* (markers) have been found which invoke Athena, and Ion and his sons (e.g. *IG* i³ 1481–99, from Aegina, Cos and Samos): it has been debated whether these are to be seen as signs of the imposition of Athenian cults on those states or of the confiscation of land there which became overseas property of sanctuaries in Athens. A sculpture group in Samos which depicted the introduction of Heracles to Olympus, perhaps set up after the war of 440–439, showed not Samos' goddess Hera but Athena with Heracles and Zeus.

We should not think of the 'manipulation', in a sinister sense, of religion to serve the purposes of the Delian League: rather, since religion pervaded every aspect of life, it will have seemed natural that the League and Athens' position at the head of it should be expressed through religion as well as in other ways.

Philosophy

Seriously different ways of thinking about the world began among the Greeks of Asia Minor, and particularly Miletus, in the sixth century. One question which preoccupied the 'Presocratic' philosophers was what the fundamental nature of the cosmos and the world was. Thales suggested that the earth floats on water – and was believed to have successfully predicted an eclipse. Anaximander argued that the origin of all things was the infinite; Anaximenes, that the fundamental principle was air. Pythagoras, who was born in Samos but migrated to southern Italy, was particularly interested in numbers and proportions (including 'Pythagoras' theorem' about the hypotenuse of a right-angled triangle, and the mathematical basis for musical pitches).

Those who adopted approaches of this kind objected to the stories about anthropomorphic gods and goddesses which are found in Greek literature from Homer and Hesiod onwards. Pythagoras was said to have seen Homer and Hesiod punished in Hades for what they said about the gods. Xenophanes, another man who migrated from the east

of the Greek world to the west, complained that Homer and Hesiod had
represented the gods as behaving in all the ways which were disgraceful
for mortals. Heraclitus of Ephesus said that Homer ought to be expelled
from the competitions and flogged; if there were gods, they were not at
all like the gods of the poets' stories. Thales believed that 'all things are
full of gods'. Xenophanes remarked that men make gods in their own
image, different races of men each make gods resembling themselves,
and if animals could draw they would draw animal gods – whereas he
believed that there is one god, who does not resemble men, and who
sees all and directs all and is unmoving. Heraclitus believed that men
pray to statues which cannot hear and cannot answer, and that the
cosmos is governed by a rational principle, *logos*.

As well as challenging the traditional gods, the philosophers
challenged traditional 'heroic' values. Xenophanes complained that
winning prizes in the competitions at festivals did not increase the
eunomie, the healthy lawful state, of the city; the wisdom which he had
was better than the strength of men and horses. Heraclitus believed that
there is one divine law from which all human laws ought to be derived,
while what actually happened was that in different places the various
rulers imposed their own will and called that 'law'.

By the time of Pericles, we encounter those later Presocratic
philosophers known as sophists. The word *sophistes* means simply
'wise man', and was applied, for instance, to the Seven Wise Men of
archaic Greece (cf. Hdt. I. 29. i: Solon and others); but it came to be
used particularly of men in the middle and late fifth century who
continued the enquiries of the sixth-century philosophers, continued
the questioning of traditional beliefs and values, and in many cases took
payment for teaching skills needed for success in public life, including
rhetoric and argument. It is sophists of this kind who are referred to by
Cleon in Thuc. III. 38. vii and by Socrates in Ar. *Nub.* 331: they came
from various cities, but many of them found Athens a congenial and
receptive place in which to work.

If traditional religion, and traditional laws and morality, were to
be rejected, what justification, if any, was there for laws and morality?

We have noticed above Heraclitus' view that there was a divine law, but in the human world rulers imposed their own will and called that 'law'. A favourite contrast of the sophists was between *physis*, nature, which cannot be other than it is, and *nomos*, law, in the sense of human enactments which have been decided by particular people in a particular context and could be decided differently by other people in other contexts. The same idea appears already in a fragment from the poet Pindar, early in the fifth century: 'Other men have other institutions (*nomima*), and each man praises his own way' (Pind. fr. 215. *a*. 2–3 Snell & Maehler). Protagoras of Abdera, in the middle of the fifth century, maintained that we cannot know whether gods exist or, if they do, what they are like, and that man is the measure of all things; but he is represented by Plato as believing that, although laws are a human convention, as opposed to *physis*, they are a good convention, enacted by the cities to train people to live as they ought (Pl. *Prt.* 326 c 6–e 1). His younger contemporary Hippias of Elis according to Plato claimed that '*nomos* is a tyrant over men and commits many acts of violence contrary to *physis*' (Pl. *Prt.* 337 c 7–d 3), but according to Xenophon he believed also that there are some unwritten universal laws which must have been prescribed by the gods (Xen. *Mem.* IV. iv. 19).

Some of the later sophists claimed that laws are bad, because they prevent men from living as *physis* would allow. Plato gives us two versions of this: first, the claim by Thrasymachus of Calchedon that justice is 'the advantage of the stronger', that is, as Heraclitus had alleged earlier, that laws are the rules imposed on each community by whoever is in power in that community (Pl. *Resp.* I. 336 B 1–354 c 3); and secondly, the view of an otherwise unknown Callicles that laws derive from a conspiracy among the weak to prevent the strong from living as they otherwise could (Pl. *Grg.* 481 B 6-505 c 8). While Democritus of Abdera maintained that one should not be more willing to do evil if nobody would know than if all men would know (*Vorsokr.* 68 B 264), an Athenian, Antiphon the Sophist (probably but not certainly to be distinguished from Antiphon the Rhetorician), wrote a work *On Truth*, which praised *physis* above laws, and advised that one should obey the laws if one was likely to be caught breaking them but not otherwise (*Vorsokr.* 87 B 34. 12–34). Better attributed to Critias, the leader of the oligarchy of the Thirty in 404–403, than to Euripides is a fragment from a play in which one character says that at first human life was uncontrolled and bestial, with no reward for the good or punishment for the bad; then men enacted laws, so that justice might be tyrant and anybody who offended was punished; then men took to committing acts of violence in secret, until some clever and wise man invented the gods, so that fear of them would deter men from offending even in secret (*Vorsokr.* 88 B 25).

To succeed in public life, in the council, the assembly and the law courts, men needed to be able to argue a case persuasively. Those who were unhappy with that kind of cleverness represented it as making the worse cause appear the better (cf. Ar. *Nub.* 99, 112–5), and indeed Protagoras is alleged to have taught that skill (*Vorsokr.* 80 A 20–1, B 6). Rhetoric as a conscious art began to develop in the late fifth century: Gorgias of Leontini in Sicily is said to have amazed the Athenians with his manner of speaking when he visited as one of a body of envoys in 427; Antiphon the Rhetorician is the first man known to have written law court speeches for clients to deliver.

Pericles associated with sophists and intellectuals, and two in particular are linked with him. The Athenian Damon was a contemporary of Pericles: he was especially interested in music and its emotional effects; he was a friend of Pericles from the 470s or 460s onwards, and his wife was probably an Alcmaeonid called Agariste, though we cannot place her in a family tree. He was said also to have been a political adviser of Pericles (in particular, he was said to have suggested the introduction of jury pay, and it is not impossible that he did that) – but the *Areopagiticus* of his, traces of which were detected in the nineteenth century, seems not to be authentic but to derive ultimately from a fourth-century dialogue by Heraclides of Pontus. He was ostracized, probably in the late 440s (four *ostraka* against him have survived): probably this was at least in part because of his connection with Pericles, but according to Plutarch it was also due to suspicion provoked by his cleverness (Plut. *Arist.* 1. vii, *Nic.* 6. i, cf. *Per.* 4. ii–iii). Another sophist linked with Pericles was Anaxagoras of Clazomenae, also a contemporary, who arrived in Athens perhaps in 456/5. He regarded mind (*nous*) as the organizing principle behind the cosmos, and he was interested in natural phenomena and physical explanations of them. Plutarch has a story of his cutting open the skull of a one-horned ram to show that it was not portentous but had a natural cause (Plut. *Per.* 4. vi–6). As we saw in Chapter 2, it is possible that the decree of Diopithes which made it an offence 'not to believe in divine things or to teach about things up in the air' was aimed at Anaxagoras and that he was prosecuted – perhaps in 437/6 and perhaps by Cleon – and then left Athens for Lampsacus. How to explain natural phenomena was a matter for discussion in the late fifth century. Thucydides noted that eclipses of the sun happen at the new moon (Thuc. II. 28), and when in 413 an eclipse of the moon at the full moon led Nicias to delay the Athenians' withdrawal from Syracuse Thucydides commented that 'he was somewhat too much inclined to divination and the like' (Thuc. VII. 50. iv). When earthquakes affected decisions in states, he did not say what combination of physical danger and divine wrath weighed on men's minds; when the plague hit Athens, he noted that the pious and the impious suffered alike, and 'no fear of the gods or law of men' had any power to restrain men from acting as they chose in the short term, because they did not fear later retribution (Thuc. II. 53).

Protagoras not only defended laws as a worthwhile institution but was prepared to write laws himself: he is said to have written laws for the Athenian colony at Thurii, in southern Italy, when that was founded *c.* 444/3 (Diog. Laert. IX. 50).

What did Pericles believe, and what did a typical Athenian of his time, if there was such a person, believe? In a passage from his funeral oration quoted above, Pericles is represented as describing festivals as 'relaxations from toil for the spirit, … contests and sacrifices throughout the year' – thus mentioning sacrifices, which often fed human beings as well as the gods, but not actually mentioning the gods (Thuc. II.

38. i). Indeed, there is no direct mention of the gods in any of Pericles' speeches in Thucydides' history, though Plutarch mentions a reference to the gods attributed to his funeral oration after the Samian war (Plut. *Per.* 8. ix). The nearest he comes to that in Thucydides is the remark in his final speech, 'We must bear blows from heaven (*ta daimonia*, "divine things") with resignation, and blows from the enemy with manliness' (Thuc. II. 64. ii). Otherwise he refers only to fortune, as in 'We are accustomed to blame fortune for whatever happens contrary to reason' (Thuc. I. 140. i); and he says of the plague, 'Happenings which are sudden, unforeseen and contrary to all reasonable expectation enslave the spirit' (Thuc. II. 61. iii). But Pericles was much involved with the public buildings, including temples, of the 440s and 430s; and we may assume that, whatever he thought about gods, about stories of anthropomorphic gods, and about human affairs and natural phenomena, he played the part that would be expected of him on the religious occasions of the city and of units in the city to which he belonged. Failure to do that would have been widely shocking, and would certainly have attracted comment.

Among the population at large there was no doubt a spectrum from those who believed very much as people had believed a century or more earlier to those who shared many of the doubts expressed by the sophists, but probably very few people openly proclaimed their disbelief, and even fewer openly refused to take part in the traditional observances. Although Thucydides does not say so, in response to the plague the Athenians perhaps established sanctuaries of Heracles Alexikakos and/or Apollo Alexikakos ('averter of evil'), though the evidence is problematic; and the healing god Asclepius was introduced to Athens in 420/19 (*IG* ii^2 4960), after the Peace of Nicias in 421 had made contact between Athens and Asclepius' sanctuary at Epidaurus easy. The mutilation of the herms and the mock celebrations of the Eleusinian mysteries in 415 caused great alarm. Thucydides places more emphasis on the political background than on the impiety, and writes of 'other mutilations of images previously by young men in drunken revelry' (Thuc. VI. 27–9, 53, 60–1; quotation 28. i), but that is consonant with his own views, and there were certainly Athenians who took the impiety very seriously. In 411 the officials of the Eleusinian cult objected strongly to proposals to recall Alcibiades from his exile for profaning the mysteries, and when he returned to Athens in 407, they were required to cancel the curse which they had pronounced on him (Thuc. VIII. 53. ii, Plut. *Alc.* 33. iii).

Pericles lived in, and played his part in, a Greek world in which the worship of the gods continued as it had done for some centuries, and stories about the gods as anthropomorphic beings continued to be told and to be revised as they were retold. That kind of worship, and those kinds of stories, could also be questioned, as they had been in the Greek world for more than a century. Athens, with its openness to a variety of influences, had a richer mixture of religious observances than other cities; and it also was probably more receptive also of critical teaching and critical thinking than many other cities. Pericles, and other Athenians, found their own ways of living with that tension.

5

Literature, Art, Architecture

Literature

One of the most important *genres* of Greek literature in the fifth century was Athenian drama, with texts written in verse, performed in competitions at festivals of Dionysus: the city Dionysia, in the spring, and the rural Dionysia in various places in Attica in the winter; also, from *c.* 440, the Lenaea, in late winter.

According to Aristotle's *Poetics*, tragedy developed out of the choral songs known as dithyrambs (*Poet.* 4. 1448 B 24–1449 A 31); an early stage in the development is attributed to Thespis, probably in the 530s, though some scholars have considered the end of the century, after the overthrow of the tyranny, more appropriate and more likely for the institution of the city Dionysia and the inclusion of tragedy in that. While the chorus remained an essential component of tragedies, the plays gradually became more dramatic, with the addition of a second and later a third actor (when there were more characters, one actor had to play more than one part; editors have tried to work out how the parts in the various plays were divided between the actors). In the city Dionysia, each playwright presented a 'trilogy' of three tragedies, followed by a more earthy satyr-play (satyrs being imaginary, wild, subhuman creatures).

Certainly tragedies were being written and performed by the beginning of the fifth century. Phrynichus wrote a play on the Persians' *Capture of Miletus* which marked the end of the Ionian Revolt in 494 (Hdt. VI. 21. ii), and a play *Phoenician Women* on the Persian War of 480–479. Themistocles, in 493/2, may well have been the archon who accepted the *Capture of Miletus* for performance, and he was the *choregos* for Phrynichus in 477/6, possibly but not certainly when *Phoenician Women* was performed (Plut. *Them.* 5. v: cf. p. 78). Phrynichus also wrote plays about the Greeks' legendary past, and that past has provided the material for all the tragedies which survive apart from what is probably the earliest, Aeschylus' *Persians* (473/2). The playwrights had considerable freedom in recasting the details of the traditional stories for their own purposes. All our surviving tragedies are by three writers: Aeschylus (who died in the 450s), Sophocles (active 469/8–407/6) and Euripides (active 456/5–407/6).

For Aristotle tragedy was 'an imitation of serious and complete action … through pity and fear achieving the purgation (*katharsis*) of such emotions' (*Poet.* 6. 1449 B 24–8); it used a story to explore issues of general significance (9. 1451 A 36–B 32), and it tended to focus on the change from good to bad fortune of a character who was not villainous but was imperfect (10–13. 1452 A 12–1453 A 30). Euripides had a particular tendency to end his plays in a way which disconcertingly suggests (at any rate to modern readers) that something must be wrong with a world in which that is how things turn out.

Ribald comic performances probably had a long ancestry, but the inclusion of comic drama in the city Dionysia is dated 488/7 or 487/6, and comedy and tragedy were added to the Lenaea together *c.* 440. The only surviving 'old comedies', from the fifth century, are all by Aristophanes and later than Pericles' death; no earlier comedy from which 'fragments' are quoted need be earlier than *c.* 450. Old comedies have a chorus, which often gives its name to the play, and which (at any rate with Aristophanes) in the middle of the play addresses the audience directly while the action is suspended. The plots are fantastic, but originate in some feature of contemporary life; well-known figures are mocked and attacked (whether the choice of victims and their treatment reflect a definite point of view of the playwright is much debated); the gods are ridiculed, but underlying religious assumptions are not undermined; cleverness and literary skill are combined with vulgar humour, often sexual or scatological. Aristophanes' surviving plays from the 420s focus on belligerence against Sparta (*Acharnians*, 425), vulgar politicians (*Knights*, 424), sophists (*Clouds*, 423), Athenian addiction to litigation (*Wasps*, 422) and peace, when the Peace of Nicias seemed to have ended the Peloponnesian War (*Peace*, 421). Politicians are inevitably among those attacked: for the comedians' treatment of Pericles, see p. 12.

The plays were performed at festivals, before large audiences (the theatre of Dionysus in Athens, as rebuilt in the fourth century, had seats for about 15,000, but the capacity of the fifth-century theatre was less). The actors, all men, wore masks to represent their characters. Taking financial and general responsibility for a set of plays was a liturgy imposed on rich citizens (cf. p. 34): Themistocles was *choregos* for Phrynichus in 477/<u>6</u> (Plut. *Them.* 5. v), and Pericles for Aeschylus, when one of his plays was *Persians*, in 473/<u>2</u> (*IG* ii² 2318. 9–11).

In recent decades Athenian drama has been studied not only as dramatic literature but also in its context as a product of and a way of engaging with the Athenian society of its time. This is in principle to be welcomed, but I am one of those who have stressed that, while of course the festivals of other cities were not exactly the same, and the plays would not be the same if they had been written in and for some other city, much of what we find in the festivals and in the plays reflects the Athenian version of Greek city society in general rather than something peculiarly Athenian and democratic.

Before the fifth century there seems to have been no Greek prose literature, but one prose form which developed impressively during the fifth century was history. Herodotus (480s–420s) was from Halicarnassus in Asia Minor, but left after involvement in political conflict; he at any rate visited Athens, and is said to have joined the Athenian colony at Thurii (cf. p. 52). His history leads up to the wars between the Greeks and the Persians between 499 and 479, but to reach that climax he provides a great deal of material on earlier history, and on geography and ethnography. The result is enjoyable to read, and reflects an intelligent and enquiring author; to judge from fragments quoted from earlier writers, it represented a great advance on what had gone before. The Athenian Thucydides (early 450s–*c.* 400) was related to Pericles' opponents Cimon and Thucydides, son of Melesias, but became a great admirer of Pericles (cf. p. 23). In contrast to the discursive Herodotus he wrote a narrowly focused history of the Peloponnesian War (with earlier material in Book I to provide a background; the narrative breaks off in 411). He used to be seen as a paragon of objective truth, but more recently he has been studied as a writer who carefully crafted his account to lead readers to see what had happened as he wanted. He was proud, perhaps at some points too proud, of his ability to elicit the truth, and he has often been seen as a model for 'serious' historians to follow.

Art

Another art form associated particularly with Athens in the fifth century is painting on fine pottery. In the sixth century Athens had come to dominate this market, first with the black-figure style (images in black paint against an unpainted background), and from *c.* 525 with the greater opportunities provided by the red-figure style (images unpainted apart from the addition of details, against a black-painted background: cf. fig. 5.1). The subjects depicted come from a wide range of traditional stories and *motifs* from contemporary life. Since pottery can be broken but cannot beyond that be destroyed, tens of thousands of decorated Athenian pots survive complete or in part, found not only in Athens but also in various places to which they were taken – particularly Italy, and within Italy particularly Spina, on the Adriatic coast north of Ravenna. Nevertheless, it has been estimated that even at the height of activity not more than five hundred men were employed at any one time in producing this pottery.

The vases have been studied not only for the artistry of the men who decorated them but also for what we can learn from the choice and treatment of subjects, and from the uses of the vases and from where

Figure 5.1 Voronezh University, Russia: Athenian red-figure *pelike*, showing Orpheus and a Thracian, by Villa Giulia Painter (*c.* 475–425: Beazley Archive no. 207206).

they travelled. Those which are most admired are the vases of the late sixth and early fifth centuries. The fifth century saw an increasing variety in poses and naturalness in depiction, but there was also a tendency towards gaudiness, and the products of the late fifth century and the fourth are less attractive to modern eyes.

Through texts we know of paintings on a larger scale, but from the fifth century none has survived. From the fourth century there are tomb paintings in Macedon and in other places on the edges of the Greek world. In buildings most figurative paintings were done not directly on the walls but on wooden panels. In the agora in Athens, the Painted Stoa (*stoa poikile*), of the second quarter of the fifth century, had scenes both from recent history and from the legendary past (Paus. I. 15. ii–iv). The Stoa of Zeus was built in the 420s, but the paintings in it mentioned by Pausanias (I. 3. iii–iv) were of the mid-fourth century. Cimon of Cleonae (*c.* 500) is said to have invented three-quarter views, and in an approach to perspective Polygnotus of Thasos and Micon of Athens, in the second quarter of the fifth century, used different ground lines and grouping of figures to indicate position within a scene. Agatharchus of Samos began scene painting for the theatre.

The prosperous and confident Athens of the fifth century was a leading commissioner of statues and buildings. Many of the famous statues are known to us not from the originals but from Roman copies of them. At the beginning of the fifth century the more adaptable hollow-cast bronze was replacing marble for free-standing statues, and the rigid nude male *kouroi* and clothed female *korai*, and other figures which like them stared directly ahead, were giving way to more naturalized figures in a greater variety of poses, though at first restrained and still somewhat stylized. The Severe Style of this period is represented by the statues of the tyrannicides Harmodius and Aristogeiton, produced in 477/6 by Critius and Nesiotes to replace the original statues taken by the Persians in 480 (Parian Marble, *FGrH* 239 A 54: cf. fig. 5.2); the Critian Boy, found on the acropolis, has been attributed to Critius on

Figure 5.2 Moscow, Pushkin Museum of Fine Art: Cast from Naples, National Archaeological Museum, Roman copies of statues of Harmodius and Aristogeiton.

stylistic grounds but is not signed. Active about the second quarter of the century was Myron of Eleutherae, whose *diskobolos* (discus-thrower: cf. fig. 5.3) explored the possibilities of a figure in action. Slightly later Polyclitus produced his *doryphoros* (spear-bearer) and worked out a 'canon' of the proportions of the parts of the human body.

Particularly associated with Pericles was the Athenian Pheidias. The building programme on the acropolis (cf. below) provided many opportunities for sculpture; according to Plutarch Pheidias was not merely the principal sculptor for the buildings but was in charge of the whole programme (Plut. *Per*. 13. vi), though contemporary evidence does not support the view that anybody was given an appointment of that kind. An early work of his was the gigantic Athena Promachos (fighting in front), towards the north-west corner of the acropolis, said to have been visible from Sunium (Paus. I. 28. ii). His masterpieces were the gold and ivory statue of Athena which the Parthenon housed, nearly 12 metres (40 feet) high, and adorned with various smaller sculptures (descriptions by Plin. *H.N.* XXXVI. 18–19, Paus. I. 24.

Figure 5.3 Rome, Museo Nazionale delle Terme: Copy of Myron's *diskobolos*.

Figure 5.4 Nashville, Tennessee: Replica of Pheidias' statue of Athena, in replica Parthenon.

v–vii: cf. fig. 5.4), and the Zeus which he subsequently produced for Olympia, and which came to be regarded as one of the Seven Wonders of the world (cf. p. 39).

The Parthenon also had a particularly extensive range of sculptures as elements of the building: pediments showing the birth of Athena from the head of Zeus and the contest of Poseidon and Athena over Athens; metopes (panels in the upper part of the architrave above the columns) showing mythical combats; and around the cella a continuous frieze. What is depicted on the frieze is normally thought to be a version of the procession to the acropolis at the festival of the Panathenaea, running in both directions from the south-west corner and culminating at the east end with the twelve Olympian deities and what appears to be the presentation of the new *peplos* brought in the procession to clothe the cult statue of Athena (or the folding of the previous *peplos*: cf. fig. 5.5), but precisely what kind of version of that procession is endlessly debated: since no ancient text even mentions the frieze (which will not have been easy to see in situ), we are left to construct an interpretation for ourselves, and no one interpretation has obtained general consent. Many of the Parthenon's sculptures were acquired from the Ottoman Empire in and after 1801 by Lord Elgin,

Figure 5.5 Parthenon: Scene with *peplos*, from east frieze.

and were bought for the British Museum in 1816: they have figured prominently in another debated issue, whether items which were acquired legitimately at the time but could not be acquired legitimately by the standards which are applied today ought to be returned to their place of origin.

One form of art rarely produced in Pericles' lifetime was the sculptured gravestone. A few families continued to cover tombs with mounds, in the archaic manner, but in general, not only in Athens but across the Greek world, burials were much more modest and gravestones much simpler between about 500 and 430 than before or after.

Buildings in and around Athens were wrecked when the Persians sacked Athens in 480 and 479. Most urgent when the Athenians returned was the rebuilding of the city walls, where a story is told of Themistocles' outmanoeuvring a Spartan attempt to prevent that (Thuc. I. 89. iii–93. ii and later texts), of people's houses, and of essential public buildings, such as the council house on the west side of the agora (unless that was not built until after the war, as has sometimes been thought). But nothing was done at first to rebuild temples on the acropolis and elsewhere. Buildings left in ruins included on the acropolis a predecessor of the Parthenon, on which work had begun in the 480s, and the 'old temple of Athena', on a site between the Parthenon and the Erechtheum, built in the sixth century either towards the end of the Pisistratid tyranny or after its overthrow. Some, but not all, versions of an oath said to have been sworn before the battle of Plataea in 479 include an undertaking to leave temples in ruins as a war memorial (Lyc. *Leocr.* 81, Diod. Sic. XI. 29. iii; but absent from R&O 88. 21–51); but I am among those who think that the Athenians would not have considered that an appropriate response to the Persians' destruction, and I suspect that, whatever may be the truth behind our texts, that clause was invented later to explain why temples had not been rebuilt promptly. More probably, it has been suggested recently, the delay is to be attributed to a shortage of skilled men able to do the work.

Some new buildings, both sacred and secular, were erected between 478 and *c.* 450. In the north-west corner of the agora, the Stoa (portico) of the *Basileus* was built before the war and repaired after (or perhaps built after); and on the west side the *tholos*, the round house used by the *prytaneis*, was built perhaps after 462/1. Themistocles is credited with a temple of Artemis Aristoboule ('of best counsel'), perhaps to the west of the agora, and Cimon with the Theseum, probably to the east of the agora, to house the skeleton which he brought back from Scyros in 476/5 (cf. p. 46), with the Painted Stoa on the north side of the agora (Plut. *Cim.* 4. vi–vii) and with the south wall of the acropolis (Plut. *Cim.* 13. v). A separate meeting place for the assembly on the Pnyx, south-west of the agora, had been built *c.* 500, with an auditorium like that of a theatre (cf. fig. 5.6), and that remained essentially unaltered until *c.* 400. There was in fact some small-scale work on the acropolis during these years.

But there is no doubt that a major building programme on the acropolis began in 447/6 (cf. p. 51 and fig. 5.7; dates are supplied by the accounts of the various supervisory boards). This gave us the Parthenon (447/6–433/2), the Propylaea, the entrance building at the west end of the acropolis (437/6–433/2), the temple of Athena Nike (victory) just outside the Propylaea (probably planned in the 440s even though not built, or at any rate not finished, until later), and the Erechtheum (begun

Figure 5.6 Pnyx: Speaker's platform (from the remodelling of the Pnyx in the second half of the fourth century).

Figure 5.7 Acropolis from south-west: Propylaea and Athena Nike to left, Erechtheum in background, Parthenon to right, Odeum of Herodes Atticus (second century AD) in foreground.

c. 420 and after an interruption completed during 409/8–405/4). Other major buildings were erected elsewhere in Athens and in other places in Attica in the second half of the century.

The Parthenon (cf. fig. 5.8), which reused much of the stone put in place for its predecessor in the 480s, is the supreme example of what

Figure 5.8 Parthenon.

had become the standard Greek temple, with a central room or rooms surrounded by a colonnade of Doric columns. It was built entirely of marble, whereas previous temples on the Greek mainland had used *poros* limestone in part or entirely; and it was larger than any other temple on the mainland, and, in particular, than the recently built temple of Zeus at Olympia. It is remarkable for its slight departures from actual regularity which enhance the visual appearance of regularity (not unprecedented, but here particularly elaborately and well done): for instance, the columns tilt slightly inwards, and they do not taper consistently from bottom to top but swell slightly in the centre. Plutarch attributes the building to Ictinus and Callicrates (Plut. *Per.* 13. vii); Ictinus was probably the designer.

The Propylaea (cf. fig. 5.9) replaced an earlier and simpler entrance building (started before the Persian sack and repaired after). It shares architectural refinements with the Parthenon, and its axis is parallel to that of the Parthenon (but in the fifth century one did not have the unimpeded view of the Parthenon from the Propylaea which one has today). It was less than completely symmetrical, partly in order not to impinge on the bastion on which the temple of Athena Nike was built; it

Figure 5.9 Propylaea.

was left unfinished at the beginning of the Peloponnesian War, and was not finished later. It had no architectural sculpture, but paintings were placed in it; and the traveller Pausanias was particularly impressed by the coffered ceiling (Paus. I. 22. iv; §§vi–vii treat the picture gallery as distinct from the Propylaea).

The temple of Athena Nike (cf. fig. 5.10) and the sculptured parapet around it were at any rate finished after Pericles' death, and the Erechtheum was certainly built after it, but probably a version at any rate of the temple of Athena Nike was included in the original plan for the acropolis formed in the 440s. The Erechtheum was built on the north side of the acropolis, on the site of Athens' Mycenaean palace of the second millennium BC. To fit the topography and the various sacred sites which it enclosed, it is highly irregular in plan; for the Caryatid porch on the south side, with female statues used as columns, there were precedents at Delphi. Both of these temples have not Doric columns but Ionic (slimmer, and with decorated capitals) – and indeed in the Parthenon there were Ionic columns inside the west room, and the continuous frieze was an Ionic feature. Some have seen a political statement in this, a distinction of the Ionian Athenians from the Dorian Spartans, but the Doric order continued to be used in other buildings,

Figure 5.10 Temple of Athena Nike.

and there is no evidence that the orders already had those names in the fifth century.

Other temples were built in Athens and Attica about the same time, including the originally misidentified 'Theseum' (in fact a temple of Hephaestus: cf. fig. 5.11) overlooking the agora from the west, and the temple of Poseidon at Sunium (where a temple had been started at the beginning of the century but not finished). The temple of Ares, rebuilt in the agora, east of the temple of Hephaestus, in the time of Augustus, has now been identified as having originally been the temple of Athena at Pallene. At Eleusis, the approximately square *telesterion* (initiation hall), larger than its archaic predecessor, was another work of the Periclean period (Plut. *Per.* 13. vii: cf. fig. 5.12). Below the acropolis to the south-east, work on a stone theatre of Dionysus had begun in the Periclean period but was abandoned owing to the Peloponnesian War, and was eventually undertaken in the third quarter of the fourth century. However, the square odeum immediately to the east of the theatre, for the musical contests at the Panathenaea, was attributed to Pericles: it was said to be both many-seated (?) and many-columned, and to have

Figure 5.11 Temple of Hephaestus, overlooking agora.

Figure 5.12 Eleusis: *telesterion.*

been an imitation of the Persian king's tent. The long walls linking Athens to Piraeus were built in the time of Pericles, and he is himself credited with the middle wall, later than the original two (cf. pp. 17, 49). The development of Piraeus as Athens' harbour town had been started by Themistocles when he was archon, in 493/2, and continued after the

Persian Wars (Thuc. I. 93. iii); the layout of the town, about the middle of the century, was attributed to Hippodamus of Miletus (Arist. *Pol.* II. 1267 в 22–3). He afterwards laid out the Athenian colony at Thurii (cf. p. 52).

However, Athenian private houses, even of rich men, were in the fifth century still fairly modest – or at least so it was claimed in the fourth century, when the ultra-rich were accused of building more palatial houses (Dem. XXIII. *Aristocrates* 207–8, III. *Olynthiac iii.* 29).

Thucydides, arguing that the physical appearance of a city was not necessarily a reliable indication of its power, wrote that if Sparta were to be deserted nobody would believe later from the remains of its buildings how powerful it had been, but in the case of Athens people would imagine that it had been twice as powerful as it actually was (Thuc. I. 10. ii). All that we know suggests that Athens did in the time of Pericles and in the last decades of the century equip itself with a more impressive range of sacred and secular buildings than any other Greek city. In the fifth century, Athens was not only politically but also culturally predominant in the Greek world: in an expression which Thucydides included in Pericles' funeral oration, Athens was 'an education to Greece' (Thuc. II. 41. i).

6

After Pericles

Democracy

As we have seen (p. 16), Cimon opposed the democratic reforms of 462/1, and there were rumours of a plot against the democracy a few years later; but on the whole for about half a century, while Athens prospered, both rich men and poor men found it good to be Athenian citizens and at any rate acquiesced in the democracy. A pamphlet on the *Athenian Constitution*, preserved with the works of Xenophon but almost certainly not by him (the author is often referred to as the 'Old Oligarch'), was probably written in the mid-420s, and takes the strange line that democracy is bad in principle, because it promotes the interests of the bad men rather than the good men, but because of the nature of Athens the democracy there is appropriate, is successful at achieving its objects, and could not easily be overthrown.

Thucydides represented Pericles as an unchallenged leader but claimed that after his death rival leaders competed to win the favour of the people. As we have seen, Pericles was not as free from challenges as Thucydides suggested; but in other respects changes have been identified after Pericles' death. From then on, most political leaders were not, as Pericles and Cimon had been, from the families which had dominated Athenian politics since the beginning of the sixth century. While some of them, such as Nicias, still behaved as leaders from the established families had done, others, such as Cleon, cultivated an ostentatiously populist style – and for them the term 'demagogue' (*demagogos*, 'people-leader') was coined. And the new politicians did not necessarily hold office year after year, as had happened previously, but relied primarily on their ability to make persuasive speeches in the assembly and the law courts. Whereas in the middle of the century the leading politicians had regularly been elected as generals, a distinction opened up (and partnerships were sometimes established) between military officers and civilian politicians: Cleon did eventually serve as general, but was first manoeuvred into doing so when he could not have expected it (Thuc. IV. 27. iii–29. ii).

The first sign of greater fragility came in 415, when Athens was about to embark on its controversial campaign in Sicily and was in a state of heightened tension (cf. below). Shortly before the expedition set sail there were religious scandals involving damage to herms (pillars with a head of the god Hermes and genitals) and mock celebrations of the Eleusinian mysteries, which according to Thucydides were seen as signs of a plot against the democracy (Thuc. VI. 27. iii, 28. ii; 53–61). If there was a plot, its aim was more probably to prevent the expedition. The expedition went ahead, but in 413 it ended in disaster; and when the democracy was no longer delivering success it became easier to challenge it. The oligarchic régime of the Four Hundred was set up in the spring of 411 (when many of the poorer citizens were at Samos with the navy and so the balance within Athens had been upset). It was originally claimed that this régime could fight the war more successfully, but in fact it tried but failed to make peace with Sparta. In the autumn of 411, it was replaced by the intermediate régime of the Five Thousand; and in 410, after a major victory demonstrated the continuing importance of the poorer citizens and the navy for Athens, the full democracy was restored. The concept of the 'traditional constitution' (*patrios politeia*) was perhaps first deployed by oligarchs but came to be used on both sides.

After defeat at Aegospotami in the Hellespont in 405, the Athenians could not continue fighting. In 404 they came to terms with Sparta, and Sparta's commander Lysander encouraged the institution of the oligarchic régime of the Thirty. That régime too lasted only for a year: democrats who had gone into exile fought their way back, and in 403 the democracy was restored. It was to be based on 'the statutes of Draco and the laws of Solon' (enacted in the late seventh and early sixth century): the democrats had succeeded in their claim that in Athens the 'traditional constitution' was democracy.

Those experiences of oligarchy were traumatic. In the fourth century, the merits of different forms of constitution could be discussed in the philosophical schools (cf. below), but for men active in politics the unpleasantness of the alternative meant that democracy had to be accepted. On the other hand, while in the second half of the fifth century anybody opposed to the democracy in its current form was liable to be considered a revolutionary and a traitor, in the fourth it became possible to profess allegiance to democracy yet at the same time to suggest that within the democracy improvements were possible. And, as far as our evidence shows, while all politicians claimed to be loyal democrats, none were ostentatiously populist in the manner of the late fifth century's demagogues (and the word 'demagogue' came to mean simply 'politician'). Not at first, but by the middle of the fourth century, changes were made which would not have been seen as democratic in the late fifth century, in particular the creation of elected offices for men with financial ability and the revival of the council of the Areopagus as a politically active body. When the democracy was overthrown again, by the Macedonians in 321, I believe that this was not because either the Macedonians or some of the Athenians were opposed to democracy as such, but because thanks to the politician Demosthenes democracy had come to be associated not only with internal freedom but also with freedom from subjection to an external master, and to the Macedonians in particular.

Empire

The early years of the Peloponnesian War confirmed that Athens was superior to Sparta at sea but Sparta was superior to Athens on land; and in those early years Athens used up its money at a rate hard to reconcile with the view attributed to Pericles by Thucydides that Athens would be able to outlast Sparta in a prolonged war. In 428/7 Mytilene on Lesbos, one of the few Delian League members still not paying tribute but providing ships, revolted. Spartan support for Mytilene was ineffective and the revolt was put down. A proposal of Cleon that all the men should be executed and the women and children enslaved was originally carried but afterwards replaced by a slightly less harsh decision which still resulted in the execution of more than a thousand men (Thuc. III. 2–18, 25–50).

In the middle of the 420s, the Athenians attempted more adventurous strategies which might be more likely to bring them positive victory. They achieved a particularly spectacular success when they occupied Pylos, on the coast of Messenia, in 425 (Thuc. IV. 2–41), though that did not enable them to do as much harm to the Spartans as they hoped and the Spartans feared. They also realized that expenditure and income needed to be brought into balance: the large and expensive naval campaigns of the war's early years were not repeated, and they raised more money from their own citizens through the property tax known as *eisphora* (Thuc. III. 19. i), and particularly in a tribute reassessment in 425 they sought to raise more money from the Delian League (*IG* i^3 71, extracts O&R 153 ~ Fornara 136).

After 425 the Athenians were less successful. Acceptance of an invitation to get involved in Sicily, in 427, had to be abandoned in 424 when Syracuse persuaded the other Greek cities there to unite in rejecting Athenian interference (passages between Thuc. III. 86 and IV. 65). An attempt to take control of Megara in 424 failed (Thuc. IV. 66–74), as did a three-pronged attack on Boeotia in 424/3 (Thuc. IV. 76–7, 89–101). From 424 to 422, an adventurous Spartan, Brasidas, won support among the cities to the north of the Aegean, in a campaign which ended in a battle outside Amphipolis in which both he and the Athenian Cleon were killed (passages between Thuc. IV. 78 and V. 13). A year's truce between Athens and Sparta was made in the spring of 423 (Thuc. IV. 117–9), and was prolonged for a time, but eventually it broke down. The deaths of Brasidas and Cleon paved the way for the

Peace of Nicias in the spring of 421, which essentially tried to revert to the situation of 431 (Thuc. V. 14–24).

Some of Sparta's allies refused to join in the peace, and there was a period of unstable alignments until in 418 at Mantinea Sparta defeated a combination of Athens, Argos and other Peloponnesian states, and was thus able to reassert its predominant position in the Peloponnese. Athens in 415 accepted another invitation to intervene in Sicily: this was opposed by Nicias and championed by Alcibiades, a relative and ward of Pericles. Nicias' stress on the difficulty of the undertaking resulted paradoxically in a larger and more ambitious expedition than had at first been envisaged. Alcibiades' involvement in that year's religious scandals (cf. above) led to his going into exile and joining the Spartans. Sparta and the other Peloponnesians sent help to Syracuse, which the Athenians were besieging; Athens sent substantial reinforcements in 413, and, partly because of bad decisions by Nicias, Athens' campaign ended in total failure. Also in 413 the Spartans sent a force to occupy Decelea, in the north of Attica, and this stayed there until the end of the war and denied the Athenians the use of their countryside all year round (Thuc. VI–VII).

The Athenians decided to fight on; but it now seemed credible that they would be defeated as it had not previously. Various Delian League members made contact with Sparta, and so too did the Persian satraps in western Asia Minor (in the late 420s Athens seems to have made a non-aggression pact with the Persians, but more recently it had been supporting a Persian rebel). The war moved to the Aegean; Athens based its navy at Samos, and on the whole succeeded in recovering its predominance among the islands but was less successful on the Asiatic mainland.

Alcibiades had fallen out with the Spartans; and by suggesting to Athenians that if he were reinstated and the democracy were replaced by an oligarchy he could persuade the Persians to support Athens instead of Sparta he helped to bring about the revolution of 411. Persia never did change to supporting Athens, though some Athenians continued for some years to hope that it would. Alcibiades rejoined the Athenian navy, which for a time acted independently of the city of Athens. After a series of victories in the region of the Hellespont and Bosporus, in 407 Alcibiades returned to Athens, where he was formally reinstated and (uniquely) given a superior position as commander in chief. But in 406, while Alcibiades was elsewhere, a subordinate was defeated at Notium, off the coast of Asia Minor, and Alcibiades withdrew into exile again. Later the same year, when the Spartans were blockading the Athenian navy at Mytilene, the Athenians made a special effort to man another fleet, which defeated the Spartans off the Arginusae islands between Lesbos and the mainland – but the weather was bad, the Athenians were unable to pick up bodies or survivors from wrecked ships, and that led to an explosion of anger and the condemnation of the generals involved in the battle (including the younger Pericles, Pericles' son by Aspasia). In 405 the Athenians were defeated at Aegospotami in the Hellespont and lost most of their ships. After that they could not continue, and in 404 they accepted Sparta's terms: Athens had to demolish the long walls and the Piraeus walls, give up all but twelve of its warships, lose all its overseas possessions, take back its exiles (mostly oligarchs from 411–410) and become a subordinate ally of Sparta. Although a change of constitution was probably not formally required, as we saw above the Spartan Lysander encouraged the institution of the oligarchy of the Thirty.

Yet that was not the end. After a year the democracy was restored. Sparta, in spite of the Persian help which had enabled it to win the war, took over the Athenian empire and started fighting against the Persians in Asia Minor. But in Greece from the mid-390s Athens joined several former allies of Sparta in a war against Sparta, and rebuilt its walls and its navy and regained some overseas possessions. Sparta turned to diplomacy, and in 387/6 obtained Persian backing for the King's Peace, by which the Greeks of mainland Asia Minor were returned to Persia and all other Greeks were to be autonomous. What that meant was decided by Sparta to Sparta's advantage, and caused such dissatisfaction elsewhere that in 378/7, exactly a hundred years after the foundation of the Delian League, Athens founded its Second League, this time to defend the freedom of the Greeks against Sparta.

In the years which followed, Sparta, Athens and Thebes each tried to gain a superior position, with Persia in the background. Sparta was overwhelmingly defeated, on land by Thebes in 371. Athens when no longer opposed to Sparta had no purpose for its League except to advance Athenian power again, but that led to the Social War (war of the allies) in 356–355, in which Athens was defeated at sea and after which the League no longer counted for much. Thebes used Delphi to have fines imposed on its enemies, Phocis and Sparta, but that provoked the seizure of Delphi by the Phocians in 356 and a sacred war for the control of Delphi. The Phocians were finally defeated in 346, but by Philip of Macedon, who had been brought into the war, and the Thebans though on the winning side were too exhausted to benefit from the outcome. In 338 a combination of Thebes and Athens was defeated by Philip at Chaeronea in Boeotia. After that he organized the Greeks in a league of his own, and from then onwards the Greek cities had to manoeuvre in a world in which the major players were the Macedonian kingdom and, in due course, the other kingdoms which were formed out of the empire conquered from the Persians by Philip's son Alexander the Great. Until the 260s Athens still tried to play the kind of role it had played in the fifth and fourth centuries, but after being defeated then in the Chremonidean War it came to terms with the new world.

Religion and philosophy

Religion, with its varieties of divinities and cults, continued on the lines familiar in the Periclean period. As with the priestess of Athena Nike (cf. p. 63), newly instituted priesthoods were open to all Athenian men or women, and at least in some cases appointment was made not for life but for one year, as with most secular appointments. New divinities and their cults continued to be welcome in Athens: for instance, the healing god Asclepius was introduced in 420/19, probably in response to the plague (cf. p. 70); the Thracian goddess Bendis already had a presence in Athens in 430/29, and probably in 413/2 a festival of Bendis in Piraeus was established, known partly because Plato's *Republic* begins by mentioning the first celebration of the festival (Pl. *Resp.* I. 327 A 1–B 1). We happen to know from an inscription that in the fourth century a community of Egyptians in Athens was allowed to acquire land for a sanctuary of Isis, and a community of Citians (from Cyprus) land for a sanctuary of Aphrodite (R&O 91 = *IG* ii³ 337 ~ Harding 111). There seems to have been a greater tendency in the fourth century for personified abstractions to be worshipped as divinities: Eirene (peace) when the King's Peace was renewed in 375/4 (Philoch. *FGrH* 328 F 151 ~ Harding 44); a cult of Demokratia (democracy) is attested in the 330s and may have existed since 403/2.

Despite the scepticism of some intellectuals, religion still mattered, probably at least a little to all Athenians, and considerably to many of them. The religious scandals of 415 had a political dimension, but they were religious scandals, and many of the Athenians will have found the misconduct seriously shocking. While there was a tendency in fifth-century Athens to think that things were now better than ever before, there was a tendency in fourth-century Athens to think nostalgically of the glories of the past. There was a particular emphasis on religion in the time of Lycurgus, the 330s–320s, and that provided opportunities both to reaffirm traditions and to make further developments: we have various laws from this period about festivals and their funding; the regaining of Oropus (disputed between Athens and Boeotia), probably in 335, led to a particular focus on the sanctuary of Amphiaraus there; and Athens and Athenians were active at the various major sanctuaries in other places in Greece. Golden statues which had been melted down for coinage towards the end of the Peloponnesian War were replaced. Religion played a prominent part in the training programme for *epheboi*, eighteen- and nineteen-year-old Athenians, which was overhauled in the 330s. Particular attention was given to the drama performed at festivals of Dionysus (cf. below).

Traditionally, there had been a distinction between gods and human beings, though some mythical figures such as Heracles were said to have one human and one divine parent, and some human beings, particularly founders of cities, could as heroes receive a lesser kind of veneration. However, mortals whose achievements were outstanding could be considered godlike, and gradually the distinction was weakened. When Athens founded Amphipolis in 437/6, the leader of the foundation, Hagnon, received veneration already in his own lifetime; but after the battle of 422 in which Cleon and Brasidas were killed Amphipolis adopted Brasidas as its founding hero instead (Thuc. IV. 102. iii, V. 11, i). After the end of the Peloponnesian War, the Spartan commander Lysander, again while still alive, received honours of a kind normally reserved for gods, including the naming of a festival after him in Samos (Duris *FGrH* 76 F 71, *ap.* Plut. *Lys.* 18. vi). Philip of Macedon towards the end of his life received honours approaching the divine. Alexander the Great towards the end of his life was acknowledged as a god by the Greeks, probably on their initiative rather than his own, and after that the rulers of the various hellenistic kingdoms received divine honours too.

The sophists continued to the end of the fifth century to challenge accepted beliefs of various kinds, and to teach the skills needed to win arguments, represented by traditionalists as making the worse cause appear the better. Their pupils tended to come from the richer strata of society, men who could afford the time to engage with the sophists and the money to pay their fees. One application of the favourite contrast between 'nature' and 'convention' was the idea that there is no absolutely right form of government for a state but different men will prefer the form of government which promotes their own different interests – and so it was considered natural for richer men to prefer an oligarchy in which they would not have to share power with the poor to the democracy in which they did. Sophists were suspected of being behind the pressure for oligarchy in 411 (though Antiphon the Rhetorician, mentioned as one of the leading men in the oligarchic movement by Thuc. VIII.

68. i–ii, is probably to be distinguished from Antiphon the Sophist: cf. pp. 67–8). The actual opinions of Socrates are extremely hard to recover from the caricature of him in Aristophanes' *Clouds* and the later representations of him to suit their own purposes by Plato and Xenophon. He stayed in Athens under the rule of the Thirty in 404–403, and was particularly suspect for having had both Alcibiades and the oligarch Critias among his pupils. He was tried and condemned to death in 399 for not recognizing the gods whom the city recognized but introducing other gods of his own, and for corrupting the young (by imbuing them with his unorthodox views: the formal charge is quoted by Diog. Laert. II. 40).

In a less confident world the philosophy of the late fifth century was too unsettling, and fourth-century philosophy stepped back from the brink and looked once more for certainties. The Athenian Plato wrote dialogues in which he explored questions about ethics and politics, knowledge and the soul, and stressed the importance of true knowledge. Aristotle, from Stagira in Chalcidice, was in Athens as a pupil of Plato from 367 until Plato died in 348/7, and again in charge of his own school from 335 to 323. He engaged in a wide range of enquiries, including natural science and rhetoric as well as what we think of as philosophy; and in many areas he worked by generalizing from a large collection of observed instances.

Among the questions which interested both Plato and Aristotle was the governance of cities. Fifth-century Greeks had distinguished monarchy (the rule of one), oligarchy (the rule of a few) and democracy (power in the hands of the people). That distinction is first attested in a poem of Pindar, perhaps of 468 (Pind. *Pyth.* ii. 86–8), and Herodotus insistently but incredibly attributed a debate over the three forms to a group of Persians in 522 (Hdt. III. 80–3 cf. VI. 43. iii). Plato (in his *Statesman*; he had a different typology in his *Republic*) and Aristotle refined that by identifying good and bad versions of each form, those which do or do not rule according to law and in the common interest. Plato looked for an ideal state: in his *Republic* one ruled by philosopher-kings, and in his *Laws* one ruled under good laws. Aristotle in his

Politics categorized and analysed various kinds of actual régime, and asked how a city ought to be organized and how revolution could be avoided, while his school compiled a collection of 158 *Constitutions*, of which only the *Athenian* survives.

Literature, Art, Architecture

Plays, both tragedies and comedies, continued to be written and performed. A stone theatre was at last built in the city (cf. below). Old plays came to be performed along with new plays: the three great tragedians of the fifth century, Aeschylus, Sophocles and Euripides, soon achieved canonical status, and in the time of Lycurgus official texts of their plays were deposited so that performers should adhere to them ([Plut.] *X Or.* 841 F). Comedy in the course of the fourth century changed from a boisterous to a quieter tone, and from public to domestic themes (such as lovers and mistaken identities): over the past century papyri have given us a substantial body of work by Menander, active from the 320s to the 290s. Actors became international stars; and Athens took to honouring actors and, in a world in which its own superiority was increasingly challenged, stressing its importance as the place where drama had begun.

History continued to be written. The Athenian Xenophon, a man of oligarchic inclinations who spent much of his life as an exile from Athens and a dependant of the Spartans, included among his works in various *genres* the *Hellenica*, an account of Greek affairs from 411 (where Thucydides' history ends) to 362; other writers also began their narratives in 411. Other forms of history developed also: in one direction local histories, including *Atthides* (histories of Athens), of which the first was written by a non-Athenian, Hellanicus of Lesbos, at the end of the fifth century; in another direction universal histories, not limited to the Greeks, of which one written by Ephorus of Cyme about the middle of the fourth century has not survived but was used in the first century BC by Diodorus Siculus.

Rhetoric, the art of speech-making in particular and effective writing more generally, developed in the century after Pericles' death. A Sicilian orator, Gorgias of Leontini, was one of the delegation which in 427 invited Athens to intervene in Sicily, and his style, involving sentences with balanced contrasted clauses, is said to have made a great impression on the Athenians (Pl. *Hp. Mai.* 282 в 4–c 1, Diod. Sic. XII. 53. ii–v); his *Encomium of Helen* and *Defence of Palamedes* survive. Athens' judicial practices, where litigants had to plead their own cases, encouraged the rise of speech writers. The habit developed of writing out and publishing speeches, and more than a hundred speeches delivered in Athens survive (mostly law court speeches, but a few assembly speeches and funeral orations) from between *c.* 420 and *c.* 320. Also handbooks of rhetoric were written, and preserved with the works of Aristotle we have his own *Rhetoric* and the *Rhetoric to Alexander* (the latter slightly earlier, and probably by Anaximenes of Lampsacus).

As we noticed above (cf. p. 77), vase painting of the late fifth and the fourth century is less attractive, at any rate to modern eyes, than that produced earlier. By the end of the fourth century that kind of decorated pottery had gone out of fashion altogether. For larger-scale painting we continue to have reports, but no actual survivals, from Athens; but, for the fourth century, paintings made directly on the walls of the royal tombs at Aegeae (modern Vergina) in Macedon give us an indication of what could be produced, with skilful composition (including perspective) and use of colour.

Sculptors produced softer and more elegant figures (Polyclitus' 'canon' of the proportions of the human body was modified in that direction by Lysippus of Sicyon), with increasing attention to the possibility of figures' being viewed from different angles. Among the leading fourth-century practitioners were two Athenians, Cephisodotus and his son Praxiteles. Whereas nude male figures were common, nude females were rare, but Praxiteles produced a naked figure of Aphrodite for Cnidus (it is said to have been rejected by the people of Cos: Plin. *H.N.* XXXVI. 20–1). Sculptured funerary monuments, rare in the first three quarters of the fifth century, came back into fashion after that, and used domestic imagery more often than military. By the end of the fourth century sculptors were producing figures which were less idealized and more recognizable as portraits.

There was some building work in Athens *c.* 400: in the agora a new council house was erected beside the old, and the old became a repository for records; the Pnyx, where the assembly met, was rebuilt and reoriented, with the audience facing south and the speakers on the platform north (Plut. *Them.* 19. vi attributed that change to the oligarchy of the Thirty, but it is unlikely that they had either the time or the interest in the assembly to do that). In the earlier part of the fourth century, we do not hear of building work, but another period of activity began *c.* 350 and gathered pace in the 330s and 320s. Among the works of that period were a stone theatre of Dionysus at last, the stadium for the athletic contests of the Panathenaea, another rebuilding of the Pnyx, and in the agora near the council house a new monument with statues of the heroes after whom Athens' ten tribes were named (whose base served as a notice board; this replaced an earlier monument located somewhere else). And, while the buildings of the Periclean period were public buildings and publicly funded, in the fourth century rich benefactors were honoured for making individual contributions (e.g. R&O 94 = *IG* ii³ 352 ~ Harding 118. 11–20).

Envoi

As I remarked above, while fifth-century Athens believed proudly that it was doing better than ever before, fourth-century Athens looked back nostalgically to a past which it perceived as greater than the present. Formally, democracy and belief in democracy continued, but there was less certainty about what democracy actually was, and earlier leaders were considered superior to current leaders (according to one's point of view, Pericles could be the last of the great leaders or the first of the inferior leaders). Athens still sought to play a leading role in the

Greek world, but its Second League could not match the Delian League, and ended in a period of decline. Religion and religious observances continued much as in the fifth century, while philosophy sought the reassurance of certainty rather than unsettling challenges. While new tragedies were written, the great tragedies of the fifth century became classics, and middle and new comedy was less rumbustious than old; history-writing proliferated, but the fourth century did not produce a Herodotus or a Thucydides. Artistic taste changed, with a decline in painted pottery, but remarkable large-scale painting (though none survives from Athens), and more realistic and virtuosic sculpture. Public buildings continued to be erected, but with rich individuals contributing to the cost, and allegedly building grand houses for themselves too.

Athens did not have the confidence and the excitement in the fourth century that it had in the time of Pericles, but in spite of the nostalgia it was still a great city with much to be proud of.

Further Reading

Several other books in this Classical World Series are of relevance to the matters discussed in this book, in particular M. Baldock, *Greek Tragedy: An Introduction* (1989); S. Blundell, *Women in Classical Athens* (1998); C. Carey, *Democracy in Classical Athens* (2nd edition 2017); N. R. E. Fisher, *Slavery in Classical Greece* (1993); R. Garland, *Religion and the Greeks* (1994); J. E. Sharwood Smith, *Greece and the Persians* (1990); S. C. Todd, *Athens and Sparta* (1996); R. A. Tomlinson, *Greek Architecture* (1989).

Periclean Athens is included in the volume devoted to classical Greece of three current series: J. K. Davies, *Democracy and Classical Greece* (Fontana History of the Ancient World. London: Fontana Press, 2nd edition 1993); S. Hornblower, *The Greek World, 479–323 BC* (Routledge History of the Ancient World. London: Routledge, 4th edition 2011); P. J. Rhodes, *A History of the Classical Greek World, 478–323 BC* (Blackwell History of the Ancient World. Chichester: Wiley–Blackwell, 2nd edition 2010).

Two books on Pericles and Athens were published in 2016 by Cambridge University Press in New York: T. R. Martin, *Pericles: A Biography in Context*; and L. J. Samons, II, *Pericles and the Conquest of History: A Political Biography*. Both are more detailed than this book. Martin emphasizes the effect on Pericles of his family background and his experiences when young (the 'context' of his title) to explain why he adopted the policies for Athens which he did; Samons stresses that Athens was already aggressive and expansionist before the fifth century, and that Pericles sought to make Athens powerful and glorious regardless of the cost in warfare and loss of life. Another more detailed book is V. Azoulay, *Pericles of Athens* (Princeton University Press, 2014; translated by J. Lloyd from the French original, *Périclès: La démocratie athenienne à l'épreuve du grand homme*, Paris: Colin, 2010). That seeks to strike a balance between eulogy and condemnation from today's standpoint, and between Pericles and the community in which he played a prominent role, and suggests that Pericles was exceptional not in the policies which he pursued but in the extent of his theorizing about them; it ends with chapters on the subsequent reception of Pericles (and concludes that we must accept that Pericles 'has no useful lessons for our times').

A. J. Podlecki, *Perikles and His Circle* (London: Routledge, 1998), as its title indicates, is focused on Pericles and prominent figures associated with him. P. A. Stadter has written *A Commentary on Plutarch's Pericles* (Chapel Hill: University of North Carolina Press, 1989), based on the Greek text; while Podlecki has produced the shorter *Plutarch, Life of Pericles: A Companion to the Penguin Translation with Introduction and Commentary* (Bristol: Bristol Classical Press, 1987; now London: Bloomsbury).

On Athens' democracy see M. H. Hansen, *The Athenian Democracy in the Age of Demosthenes* (Bristol Classical Paperbacks. London: Duckworth, now Bloomsbury, 2nd edition 1999), but note that this book's main focus is on the third quarter of the fourth century and that some of the statements made in it are not generally agreed but controversial. On Athens' empire as understood half a century ago see R. Meiggs, *The Athenian Empire* (Oxford University Press, 1972); problems are briefly surveyed by P. J. Rhodes, *The Athenian Empire* (*Greece and Rome* New Surveys in the Classics xvii, 2nd edition 1993); some newer approaches are offered by J. Ma et al. (eds), *Interpreting the Athenian Empire* (London: Duckworth, now Bloomsbury, 2009).

On Athenian religion see R. C. T. Parker, *Athenian Religion: A History* (Oxford University Press, 1996); *Polytheism and Society at Athens* (Oxford University Press, 2005). On the sophists see G. B. Kerferd, *The Sophistic Movement* (Cambridge University Press, 1981); fragments are translated by K. Freeman, *Ancilla to the Pre-Socratic Philosophers* (Oxford: Blackwell, 1948) and (a selection with annotations) by R. A. H. Waterfield, *The First Philosophers: The Presocratics and Sophists* (Oxford World's Classics. Oxford University Press, 2000). On Greek literature in general see P. E. Easterling and B. M. W. Knox (eds), *The*

Cambridge History of Classical Literature, i. *Greek Literature* (Cambridge University Press, 1985); on tragedy and Athens, D. M. Carter (ed.), *Why Athens?* (Oxford University Press, 2011); on comedy and Athens, D. M. MacDowell, *Aristophanes and Athens* (Oxford University Press, 1995). On Greek art in general see C. M. Robertson, *A History of Greek Art* (Cambridge University Press, 1975); *A Shorter History of Greek Art* (Cambridge University Press, 1981); on pottery, B. A. Sparkes, *Greek Pottery* (Manchester University Press, 1991); on fifth-century sculpture, J. Boardman, *Greek Sculpture: The Classical Period* (London: Thames & Hudson, 2nd edition 1991); on the buildings of Periclean Athens, T. L. Shear, Jr., *Trophies of Victory: Public Buildings in Periklean Athens* (Princeton University Press for Princeton University Department of Art and Archaeology, 2016).

The most authoritative single-volume encyclopaedia of the Graeco-Roman world is S. Hornblower and A. J. S. Spawforth with E. Eidinow (eds), *The Oxford Classical Dictionary* (Oxford University Press, 4th edition 2012; a 5th edition is being produced on line). R. J. A. Talbert (ed.), *Barrington Atlas of the Greek and Roman World* (Princeton University Press, 2000), is austerely limited to topographical maps of larger and smaller regions; N. G. L. Hammond (ed.), *Atlas of the Greek and Roman World in Antiquity* (Park Ridge, NJ: Noyes, 1981), includes also maps focused on themes, battles and particular periods.

Index

Athens and Sparta, Pericles, Plutarch and Thucydides (son of Olorus, the historian) occur on many pages and have not been indexed. Men and women who are indexed are Athenian unless otherwise stated.